Law Questions & Answers

COMPANY LAW

Questions and Answers Series

Titles in the Series

'A' Level Law
Company Law
Constitutional and Administrative Law
Conveyancing
Criminal Law
EC Law
English Legal System
Equity and Trusts
Family Law
Land Law
Landlord and Tenant
Law of Contract
Law of Evidence
Law of Torts
Wills, Probate and Administration

Other titles in preparation

Law Questions & Answers

COMPANY LAW

Second Edition

S. KUNALEN

*LLB (Hons) (London), LLM (London) (Mark of Distinction)
Barrister of Lincoln's Inn, Advocate and Solicitor, Singapore
formerly Principal Lecturer in Law at Advanced Law Tutors,
Singapore*

SUSAN McKENZIE

*MA, LLM (London), MSI Arb,
Barrister of Inner Temple, Advocate and Solicitor,
formerly Principal Lecturer in Law at Advanced Law Tutors,
Singapore*

BLACKSTONE
PRESS LIMITED

Published by
Blackstone Press Limited
Aldine Place
London W12 8AA
United Kingdom

Sales enquiries and orders
Telephone +44-(0)-20-8740-2277
Facsimile +44-(0)-20-8743-2292
e-mail: sales@blackstone.demon.co.uk
website: www.blackstonepress.com

ISBN 1-84174-095-0
© S. McKenzie, S. Kunalen 2001
First published 1996
Second edition 2001

British Library Cataloguing in Publication Data
A catalogue record for this book is available from the British Library

Typeset in 10/12pt Times
by Montage Studios Limited, Tonbridge, Kent
Printed and bound in Great Britain by M & A Thomson Litho Ltd,
East Kilbride

Contents

Preface

In teaching the subject of Company Law over the years we have come to find that the greatest difficulty encountered by students is their ability to deal with the volume of cases and legislative provisions that the subject of Company Law has generated over the years.

In dealing with a Q & A book of this nature what we have set out to do is to deal with key issues that are likely to be tested in essay and problem-type questions. In this way it is hoped that this will help the student preparing for an exam to have a sense of direction when revising the topics.

We have also found that although the subject is interesting and students can relate to it, it is when revising for examinations that difficulties may be encountered. Further this Q & A will sharpen your examination technique and your understanding of Company Law.

This book should be used in conjunction with the text book and a case book. The books that we recommend would be Blackstone's Company Law and Blackstone's case book on Company Law.

While the purpose of this Q & A is to guide the student concerning the key issues raised it is not a substitute for consistent work throughout the academic year and we advise students to start their studies and revision as early as possible.

This book is suitable for students preparing for all company law examinations, whether law degree, business studies or accounting qualifications. It is written at degree level and professional level standard but it is also suitable for post-graduate level.

We would like to thank Alistair MacQueen and Heather Saward for all their assistance and encouragement. We are also grateful for Mr Derek French's helpful comments. Further, we would also like to thank Susan's mother, her mother's husband and her family for all their support over the years.

Finally, we would like to thank all the students that we have taught over the years. It has all been great.

Susan McKenzie and S. Kunalen
September 2000

Table of Cases

Table of Statutes

Table of Secondary Legislation

1 Introduction

THE PURPOSE OF THIS BOOK

The purpose of this Q & A book is to give students greater confidence and guidance when answering questions in company law.

There are two aspects to the study of law:

(a) To develop a sound understanding of the law.

(b) To be able to apply that law to answering questions.

This is where the Q & A book comes to your aid: to help you develop the skills of application to exam questions.

THE IMPORTANCE OF USING ONLY RELEVANT INFORMATION IN EXAMS

We have always taught our students that the examiner has taken a lot of time and effort to devise the questions on the exam paper. He has an ego, he has a face. He wants you to answer his question, not give some prepared answer.

Therefore the examiner's questions are more important than all the knowledge that you have built up over your course of study.

Your function is to behave like a computer in the sense of accessing the relevant information and apply only that to the question. The rest of your knowledge is like a databank. It is your store of knowledge, there to be tapped and used when it is needed. If it is not relevant then you must resist the temptation of using it in the exam. That knowledge is not irrelevant, it is the store of knowledge that you should be developing throughout your studies for use in your future career.

Ironically if you display all your knowledge in the exam, then that will result in the examiner believing that you are answering your own question and not his question. It is at this stage that you will not excel in terms of exam marks.

The secret to exam success is accessing only the relevant knowledge to answer the question and then adding to that knowledge by commenting critically on it.

THE IMPORTANCE OF TIME MANAGEMENT

Another fault of students is to mismanage time in the exams. Whatever happens you must answer the required number of questions and if you concentrate on relevant issues only then you will manage your time properly. The examiner will then be on your side and will reward you accordingly.

Further you should note that in company law the examiners generally reward you for intellectual stamina and resilience, i.e., you are the student who keeps arguing and attempting the questions even though the issues are demanding.

2 Corporate Personality

INTRODUCTION

Corporate personality is a very important topic from the company law exam point of view. Further it is the foundation for the rest of your study of company law.

Therefore you need to understand the nature of the separate corporate personality and you need to explain what this means.

This area can be tested as either an essay question or a problem question.

The main point to note about corporate personality is that a new entity is created when a company is incorporated. As this creation is a new entity then it is treated as a distinct and separate personality from the shareholders (who are also known as the members). As a result of this a veil of incorporation is created which generally cannot be lifted unless one of the exceptions created by the case law or by statute applies. The original reason for the creation of a separate legal personality was to divorce the company's liability from its members. In fact this is a major advantage of incorporation of a company.

Your studies, for exam purposes, should concentrate on the following areas:

(a)   A consideration of all the possible reasons for which the court will lift the veil of incorporation. Then specific areas should be considered such as:

(i)   when the members can be held liable for the company's debts,

(ii)   when the parent company will be liable for the debts of the subsidiary company.

(b)   The major legislative enactments have to be considered, namely, sections 213 to 215 of the Insolvency Act 1986. The legislative intent behind such provisions has to be analysed.

QUESTION 1

The company is an association of its members and a person separate from its members. Discuss.

Commentary

This question requires a discussion of *Salomon* v *A. Salomon & Co. Ltd* [1897] AC 22. This would include the approach of both the Court of Appeal and the House of Lords in that case. You should be familiar with the case as it is fundamental for understanding the principles upon which company law is based. It would then be necessary to study systematically the important consequences of incorporation which have been elaborated in the answer.

Suggested Answer

The statement in the question expresses the legal position set out in the House of Lords decision in *Salomon* v *A. Salomon & Co. Ltd*. Mr Salomon had conducted his bootmaking business as a sole trader and he sold it to a company incorporated for this purpose. The name of the company was A. Salomon & Co. Ltd. Salomon was the main shareholder and the other members were his wife, his daughter and four sons.

The minimum number of seven members, as required under the then companies legislation was satisfied. The business was sold to the company for over £39,000. The company issued part of the purchase price in the form of debentures, and he subscribed for 20,000 £1 shares. Mr Salomon was granted a floating charge over the company's assets. The company subsequently went into liquidation.

The liquidator had resisted Salomon's claim to enforce the charge on the company's assets by arguing that Mr Salomon was in reality running the business as his own and that therefore he should be responsible for the debts of the company. At first instance the judge concluded that the company had conducted the business as agent for Mr Salomon and he was responsible for the debts. The Court of Appeal held that the company incorporated by Mr Salomon was incorporated contrary to the true intent and meaning of the Companies Act 1862. Therefore the Court of Appeal was prepared to treat the company as being a trustee for Mr Salomon and as such Mr Salomon had to indemnify the company. At the House of Lords stage, the House of Lords held that Mr Salomon had merely taken advantage of the Companies Act to do business as enabled by the Act and there was no fraud. Lord Macnaghten went on to state that on incorporation a company at law is a different person altogether from the subscribers to the memorandum and that even if the business was conducted by the same persons as before incorporation, the company is in law not the agent of the subscribers or trustee for them.

Lord Halsbury stated that the company, when legally incorporated, must be treated like any other independent person with rights and liabilities appropriate to itself.

We now have to consider the consequences flowing from the company's position as a separate person.

The Property of the Company

In *Macaura* v *Northern Assurance Co. Ltd* [1925] AC 619, the owner of a business had sold his business to a company and he owned almost all the shares.

The insurance policy concerning the company's property was in Macaura's own name. He had not transfered the insurance policy to the company. The company's property was then destroyed.

Macaura's claim that he had an insurable interest did not succeed. In the House of Lords, Lord Wrenbury stated that a corporator, even if he holds all the shares, is not the corporation. The position that was confirmed was that neither a member of the company nor a creditor has any property, legal or equitable, in the assets of the corporation.

The Company's Ability to Enter into Contracts

The company, by being a separate legal personality, can enter into transactions not only with other third parties but also with the members themselves. In *Lee* v *Lee's Air Farming Ltd* [1961] AC 12, the Privy Council was concerned with the plaintiff's husband who was a controlling shareholder and was a governing director of the company in that capacity. The plaintiff's husband was killed in an air crash while carrying out the company's crop-spraying business. The Privy Council held that the deceased and the company were separate legal personalities and it was possible for the deceased to enter into an employment contract with the company.

The Company's Decision of a General Meeting and the Position of a Company as a Separate Legal Person

In *Northern Counties Securities Ltd* v *Jackson and Steeple Ltd* [1974] 1 WLR 1133, the defendant company had failed to fulfil its obligations under a contract and had been ordered by the court to perform those obligations. The company was required by the Stock Exchange to obtain its members' approval before performing the contract. The directors had overlooked the issue of obtaining the consent of the shareholders.

The court was not prepared to grant an order whereby the members were required to vote in favour of the company performing its obligations. A failure on the part of the company to fulfil its obligations would be contempt on the part of the company and not the members.

Perpetual Succession

The company being an artificial legal personality would have perpetual succession. That is, even if there is a change in membership as a result of a member dying or if there is any mental or physical incapacity the company could still continue to do business.

Corporate Personality Enables the Property of the Association To Be More Clearly Defined

On incorporation the corporate property belongs to the company and its members have no direct property rights to it. The members merely have shares in the undertaking. In *Short* v *Treasury Commissioners* [1948] 1 KB 116, Evershed LJ referred to shareholders being not part owners of the undertaking and their interest in the undertaking being something different from the totality of the shareholdings. This would mean that any change in membership would not affect the company's property. This would contrast with the position of partnerships where change in the constitution of the partnership firm would cause dissolution of the partnership firm.

Transferable Shares

The separation of the business from its members ensures that members have the freedom, subject to the articles of association, to transfer shares. In the case of partnerships, a partner would be able to assign his interest to an assignee, who would be entitled to receive what the firm distributes in respect of the partnership share. The original parties would be still liable as far as existing liabilities are concerned. The only way a partner can be relieved of liabilities as a partner is when the creditors agree expressly or impliedly to release him.

In conclusion, it will be seen from the consequences of incorporation that the limited company offers potential advantages in respect of doing business in a way a sole proprietorship or a partnership would not be able to offer. But at the same time it must be noted that the consequences of the *Salomon* case do bring about a separation of assets and control over the business, in the sense that even a majority shareholder cannot claim any interest in the assets of the company.

QUESTION 2

Dr Fleece, after many years of researching into natural cures, set up a company, Silver Fleece Ltd. The nominal capital was £100 which was divided into 100 £1 shares of which one was held by his wife. Although the business run by Dr Fleece was worth £50,000 it was transferred to the company for £80,000. The company in exchange for the business issued Dr Fleece with a debenture for £80,000 secured by a fixed charge on the company's collection of crystals, precious stones and antique books.

In January 1999 a fire damaged the premises of the business. Dr Fleece was unable to attend to many of his patients and had suffered a loss of a month's business resulting in a loss of £2,000. There was also physical damage that resulted in a loss of £10,000. Dr Fleece had effected insurance cover in respect of loss of business and the damage to the premises. However, on incorporation he had failed to assign the insurance policy to the company.

In late 1999 Dr Fleece was advised by his accountant that due to a fall in demand for natural medicine and also because there have been adverse media campaigns warning people of the dangers of natural cures, something had to be done to prevent the company going into insolvency. Dr Fleece ignored this advice and continued to trade believing that the company would return to solvency.

It also emerged that a few hundred people became seriously ill as a result of consuming tablets sold by the company. The claim for damages will be in the region of a few hundred thousand pounds.

The company was wound up recently on a petition of one of the creditors and on the grounds of the company being unable to pay its debts and a liquidator has been appointed.

Discuss.

Commentary

The question is one where the area of corporate personality and the lifting of the veil is tested in a practical way. The question is also deliberately vague in some areas and requires a consideration of different possibilities.

Suggested Answer

Charge in Favour of Dr Fleece for £80,000 Secured on the Company's Assets

The first concern of the liquidator would be the amount for which the business was transferred to the company. The facts indicate that the business was worth only £50,000. In the leading case of *Salomon* v *A. Salomon & Co. Ltd* [1897] AC 22, the company had also paid much more for the business and the assets of Aron Salomon. However, the House of Lords treated the valuation as reflecting the expectations of Salomon as opposed to any true valuation and was not able to identify any fraud.

On our facts it is not clear why Dr Fleece decided to incorporate a company with limited liabilty. However, the House of Lords in *Salomon* proceeded to hold that an individual could utilise the corporate structure to his advantage and so long as the requirements of the Companies Act are complied with then the law will recognise the company.

In the opinion of Lord Herschell even if other shareholders (in this case Dr Fleece's wife) are 'dummies' or a nominee of Dr Fleece, the company would be treated as a properly constituted corporation.

As for the effect of the Insolvency Act 1986, the facts do not indicate when the company was incorporated, but it has to be noted that a charge created in certain circumstances could be set aside by section 239, if the company during the 'relevant time' does any act to prefer the particular creditor, so that he would be in a better position than he would have been if the thing had not been done. The 1986 Insolvency Act by section 240 provides for a period of two years ending with the time the winding up petition was presented if the creditor is a 'connected' person. Section 249 of the Act defines a 'connected' person as including a director of the company. In this case, Dr Fleece would come within the definition.

The liquidator can, if here there is a preference, apply to the court for an order stating what the position would have been if the company had not given that preference.

The Fire in January 1999 and Possible Claims on the Insurance Policy

The principle in *Salomon*'s case would dictate that on incorporation the company is a separate legal personality from its members and that if the insurance policy is in Dr Fleece's name then he can make a claim only if he has an insurable interest.

Dr Fleece would not be able to argue that, since he holds the majority shares, he should have an insurable interest in the premises.

In *Macaura* v *Northern Assurance Co. Ltd* [1925] AC 619, the House of Lords held that no shareholder has any right to any item of property owned by the company as the shareholder has no legal or equitable interest. The shareholder, according to the House of Lords, is only entitled to share in the profits of the company while it continues to carry on business and a share in the distribution of the surplus assets when the company is wound up.

The decision of *Macaura* v *Northern Assurance Co. Ltd* is a very harsh application of the principle of *Salomon*. As for the loss of the business, even though Dr Fleece is a majority shareholder the loss of the business as a result of the fire damage would also be damage that would be treated as being suffered by the company. However, it could be argued, and the point did not directly arise in *Macaura*, that it would be possible to calculate the loss of business which would affect Dr Fleece directly as opposed to calculating the interest in the property. However, the *Macaura* decision would seem to determine the matter conclusively, that is, a shareholder, even a shareholder who holds all the shares, would be treated as not having an interest in the company's business or assets.

Negligence Claims Against the Company

Turning now to the liability created by the company having sold tablets to the public, which has created liability in negligence. Relying on the principle in *Salomon* the company would be liable for any negligence that has arisen. This would mean that the plaintiffs in any action against the company cannot proceed to establish liability against Dr Fleece personally.

There are two ways in which personal liability can be established against an individual director or a managing director. The first is on the basis that the company is a 'sham' such as in *Jones* v *Lipman* [1962] 1 WLR 832. Here the court held that the company can be disregarded if it is a 'sham' or a 'device' which is used as a mask which is held before a shareholder.

In *Jones* a defendant to avoid specific performance when he was in breach of contract, incorporated a company with a nominal capital and transferred the property to the company.

The other way in which a court would consider personal liability on the part of a director is if liability can be established for negligent misstatement. The liability based on negligent misstatement can be established if it can be shown that a director had assumed personal responsibility for a company's negligent advice or performance of some service.

In the House of Lords decision of *Williams* v *Natural Life Health Foods Ltd* [1998] 1 WLR 830 the House of Lords refused to hold an individual, who controlled a company, personally liable for statements in a brochure even though he had the relevant expertise in the field.

Turning to our facts, the real motives of Dr Fleece when he decided to incorporate the company are not clear. However, even if he intended to avoid liabilities and to limit his liability only to the nominal capital that he has contributed, the law, as held in *Adams* v *Cape Industries plc* [1990] Ch 433, permits a shareholder to take advantage of the efficacy of the company. The Court in *Adams* went on to state that only if there is some illegality involved such as in *Jones*, would the company be treated as a sham.

It would appear here that if Dr Fleece has used the company lawfully to realise his liability then there is nothing that the law can do, unless legislation provides for personal liability.

Since the claim against the company is in negligence and not in negligent misstatement the issues arising in the case of *Williams* do not directly arise here. Further, a court would not be prepared to consider any aspect of control by Dr Fleece of his company since no direct personal relationship arises between the claimants and Dr Fleece.

Section 214 of the Insolvency Act 1986

By section 214 of the Insolvency Act 1986 the liquidator can apply to the court to make a director liable to contribute towards the company's assets on a winding up. The liquidator would have to prove that the directors knew or ought to have known that there was no reasonable prospect of the company avoiding going into insolvent liquidation.

The court would have to consider the factors in section 214(4) of the Act which not only allows the general knowledge, skill and experience of the director but also what steps a reasonably diligent person having the experience of the director would have taken.

In *Re Produce Marketing Consortium Ltd (No. 2)* [1989] BCLC 520, the court was concerned in seeing what a director had done at some point when it had become known that the company could not avoid insolvent winding up. Here Dr Fleece believed that the company could return to solvency but there is no indication of what particular measures had been taken to achieve this. The objective standard would be considered in terms of what a reasonably prudent director would have done. If there is liability for wrongful trading then as compensation the court can decide how much a director would have to contribute towards the company's assets. The court has to decide how much the company's assets have depleted as a result of the director's conduct.

QUESTION 3

To what extent have the attitudes of the courts changed in respect of piercing the veil? Do the decisions of the courts in this area show any consistent principles? Discuss.

Commentary

In this question you should show how the attitudes of the courts have changed, particularly in recent cases in respect of recognising exceptions to the *Salomon* principle.

A good approach here is to deal with the analysis of the law by the Court of Appeal in *Adams* v *Cape Industries plc*. One should consider a critique of the *Adams* decision. Also the answer should go on to consider if there are any consistent principles. One needs to consider the possible conflict between the *DHN* case (*DHN Food Distributors Ltd* v *Tower Hamlets London Borough*

Council [1976] 1 WLR 852), and the *Woolfson* decision (*Woolfson* v *Strathclyde Regional Council* 1978 SC (HL) 90). The essential question that you should consider in your studies is: what are the circumstances under which a parent company should be responsible for the debts of a subsidiary? You should also note that the material covered here can be tested in problem-type questions as well.

Suggested Answer

In examining the first part of the question which concerns the extent to which the attitudes of the courts have changed, the effect of *Salomon* v *A. Salomon & Co. Ltd* has to be considered. The House of Lords' decision in *Salomon* had established as a basic principle that a company, even if it is a 'one-man company' such as in *Salomon*, cannot be a mere alias or an agent of the principal shareholder. This would mean that whatever the economic realities, the law begins with the principle of the company being a separate legal entity.

In *Lee* v *Lee's Air Farming Ltd* [1961] AC 12, the New Zealand Court of Appeal held that a widow was not entitled to claim compensation from the insurers of the company on the basis that the deceased was an employee of the company. The difficulty here was that the deceased was the governing director of the company and he beneficially owned all the shares. He was also appointed as chief pilot. The New Zealand Court of Appeal took the stand that it was not possible for the deceased to be an employee as he could not give himself instructions. The Privy Council reversed the decision on the basis that in law the deceased Lee was a distinct personality from the company. In the view of the Privy Council the deceased Lee in his capacity as a director could enter into a contract on behalf of the company, with himself, as an individual. In the opinion of L. C. B. Gower, *Gower's Principles of Modern Company Law*, 5th ed. at p. 125, '... the magic of corporate personality enabled him to be master and servant at the same time'.

While *Lee* v *Lee's Air Farming Ltd* represents a strict application of the principle in *Salomon*, in recent years, particularly in the 1970s and the mid-1980s the English courts had shown a willingness to depart from the *Salomon* decision whenever it was necessary to achieve justice.

In the Court of Appeal decision of *DHN Food Distributors Ltd* v *Tower Hamlets London Borough Council* (*DHN*), the issue related to the question of whether DHN Food Distributors Ltd could claim compensation for business disruption when the land on which it was carrying on business was compulsorily acquired.

The difficulty was that the land was owned by a wholly owned subsidiary, Bronze Investments Ltd.

The structure of the companies was such that *DHN* was the holding company which carried on the business of the company where the other wholly owned subsidiaries provided the vehicles used in the business, and Bronze Investments Ltd provided the land on which the business was carried out.

To Lord Denning MR there was a tendency of the courts to disregard the separate legal personality of the companies within the group. Here Lord Denning had relied on a passage from Professor Gower's work, *Principles of Modern Company Law*, 3rd ed. (1969). Professor Gower in the passage referred to the House of Lords decision of *Harold Holdsworth & Co. (Wakefield) Ltd* v *Caddies* [1955] 1 WLR 352. In this case Caddies had been appointed managing director of Holdsworth & Co, the parent company of the group. It was argued that he could not be ordered to devote his whole time solely to duties in relation to the affairs of the subsidiaries as they were separate legal entities. The House of Lords rejected this argument and went on to hold that the service agreement with Caddies should be interpreted in the light of the facts and realities, which would mean that in commercial terms the parent and the subsidiaries should be treated as a single economic entity.

The significance of the *DHN* case was that Lord Denning did not base his reasoning on the interpretation of any relevant legislation. Lord Denning based his reasoning purely on the 'single economic unit argument' and treating the relationship between the group of companies like that of a partnership of all three companies. It was on this basis that Lord Denning proceeded to conclude that all three companies should be treated as one and that the parent company should be recognised as that one company for the purposes of compensation for business disruption.

The approach taken by Lord Denning was to ignore the technical point of the companies within the group being separate legal entities. The view was also taken in an earlier decision of *Scottish Co-operative Wholesale Society Ltd* v *Meyer* [1959] AC 324. In that case it had been argued that the appellant could not have conducted the affairs of the company in a manner that was oppressive to some part of the members within the meaning of the then section 210 of the Companies Act 1948, since it was not the appellant but its subsidiary that had carried out the acts complained of. The House of Lords had not accepted this technical point, since the policy of the subsidiary was dictated by the parent.

It could therefore be argued that in recent years there has been a tendency to disregard separate legal personality whenever it was considered convenient to do so, particularly when the realities in the opinion of the court justified it. But in the Court of Appeal decision of *Adams* v *Cape Industries plc*, we find a different attitude where there was a greater reluctance to depart from the corporate separate legal entity principle. The court in *Adams* had to deal with the issue of whether judgments obtained in the United States against an English registered company, Cape, could be enforced in the United Kingdom. This depended on whether Cape could be said to have been 'present' in the United States. The court held that the English courts will not treat a trading corporation as incorporated under the law of one country as present within the jurisdiction of another unless:

(a) it has established and maintained at its own expense a fixed place of business there and for more than a minimal time carried on its business there through its servants and agents, or

(b) its representative has for more than a minimal time been carrying on its business there from some fixed place of business.

To establish that Cape had been present in the United States the following arguments were relied on by the plaintiffs:

(a) 'the single economic unit' argument.

(b) the 'corporate veil' point and the agency argument.

On the 'single economic unit' argument the *Holdsworth* and the *DHN* cases were relied upon.

The Court of Appeal came to the conclusion that the *DHN* case is to be regarded as a case based on the interpretation of the relevant statutory provisions of compensation. The Court of Appeal also was of the view that the correctness of the *DHN* case was doubted by the House of Lords in *Woolfson* v *Strathclyde Regional Council*. It is submitted that in the *DHN* case Lord Denning did not consider himself as involved in the interpretation of any particular statutory provision.

As for the corporate veil point the Court of Appeal was of the view following the *Woolfson* decision that the corporate veil can only be disregarded if the corporate structure is a 'mere façade' concealing the true facts. The Court of

Appeal, having considered *Jones* v *Lipman* [1962] 1 WLR 832, concluded that the motives of the architects of the façade were highly relevant. The Court of Appeal found that a wholly owned subsidiary, AMC, was a façade whereby Cape used AMC as a corporate name on its invoices so that it could continue to sell asbestos in the United States of America, reducing if not eliminating the appearance of the involvement of Cape. In the final analysis what mattered most to the Court of Appeal was whether the subsidiary AMC had its own place of business in the United States or whether it was the business of Cape. On this it was found that AMC was an independent corporation which had its own chief executive and was carrying on its own business and not that of Cape.

The Court of Appeal acknowledged that Cape could use a corporate structure to ensure that the legal liability in respect of particular or future activities of the group fell on one member of the group as opposed to another. The Court of Appeal was not prepared to accept the argument that Cape had organised the affairs in such a way as to benefit from the group's asbestos trade without the risks of tortious liability.

As to the agency agreement, the Court of Appeal found that in the absence of any express agreement as to agency there is no presumption of a relationship of agency. One at this stage finds that a court today would only be prepared to depart from the principle of separate legal personality in the following circumstances, namely, if there is a question of construction of a contract such as in the *Holdsworth* case or statutory provision such as in the *DHN* case where one is concerned with the statute dealing with compulsory acquisition. The second situation is where the court is satisfied that the company is a 'mere façade' concealing the true facts. It is here there is little guidance from the Court of Appeal in the *Adams* v *Cape Industries plc* decision, although the motive of the incorporators was thought to be highly relevant. The third situation is where it can be established that a company is the agent of its creditors or its members, whether it is a corporate or natural person.

It is also necessary to note that in *Adams* v *Cape Industries plc* the court was not concerned with the approach, particularly of Lord Denning, of departing from the *Salomon* principle whenever it was in the interests of justice. However, in the area of conducting legal proceedings a court may disregard the separate corporate personality if it is the only practical way of conducting proceedings. In *Creasey* v *Breachwood Motors Ltd* [1993] BCLC 480, Mr Creasey had sued his former employers Breachwood (Welwyn) Ltd for breach of contract of employment. Default judgment was entered against Breachwood Ltd in the sum of over £60,000. The directors of Breachwood Ltd had unknown to Mr Creasey transferred all the assets and liabilities to another company, Breachwood Motors Ltd, and paid off Breachwood's trade debtors, so as to maintain its creditworthiness. However, Breachwood did not have sufficient assets to meet Mr Creasey's claim and the company was later wound up and struck off the register.

The deputy High Court judge had been prepared to substitute Breachwood Motors Ltd as a defendant in the action. This was done as the court found that the cost of Mr Creasey suing the directors, or restoring Breachwood Ltd to the register and then putting the company into liquidation to enable the liquidator to pursue the claim against the directors, would result in costs being greater than what Mr Creasey would recover.

The decision in *Creasey* has to be now viewed in the light of the Court of Appeal decision of *Ord v Belhaven Pubs Ltd* [1998] 2 BCLC 447. In that case Belhaven was a subsidiary company which owned a pub. In 1989 Mr & Mrs Ord relying on Belhaven's optimistic claims regarding the turnover and profitability of the business bought a 20 year lease of the pub and at a substantial cost attempted to promote the pub's business. However the business of the pub failed. The Ords then issued a writ against Belhaven claiming their losses. In 1992 and 1995 Belhaven restructured the group thereby transferring assets from Belhaven to a co-subsidiary and then to a holding company. The transfers were made for consideration and at book value. The plaintiffs then in 1997 applied to court to substitute the holding company and another co-subsidiary as defendants in place of Belhaven.

Although the plaintiffs succeeded at first instance, on appeal the Court of Appeal refused to allow the substitution of the defendants under the Rules of the Supreme Court. On the aspect of lifting the veil the Court of Appeal concluded that there was no evidence that any assets had been transferred at undervalue nor was there any improper motives for the transactions.

Hobhouse LJ doubted the correctness of *Creasey* on the principle of piercing the corporate veil. Hobhouse LJ concluded that the judge at first instance treated the group of companies as a single economic unit, an approach that cannot today be supported in view of the Court of Appeal's review of authorities in *Adams v Cape Industries plc* [1990] Ch 433.

In conclusion, it is submitted that there are no consistent principles that can be discussed in dealing with the disregarding of the corporate personality.

QUESTION 4

C plc is a large multinational corporation registered in the UK. It has branches and subsidiaries in various countries which specialise in the manufacture of cheap and economical motor vehicles specially tailored to deal with the problems of urban driving. Some two years ago C plc established a subsidiary with a paid-up capital of £1,000 to develop the electrical components of a new type of car that would automatically navigate the car to pre-set destinations. The subsidiary D Ltd was financed by another subsidiary E Ltd which is in the business of marketing C plc's cars in the UK and Europe. The business premises of the subsidiaries in the UK are owned by E Ltd. Recently D Ltd designed the automatic navigation system for the new type of car, however there was a design defect resulting in numerous serious accidents, with claims running into millions of pounds.

Also recently the local authority in the area where D Ltd was carrying on its business, had compulsorily acquired the business premises and the local authority is only prepared to offer compensation to E Ltd for its business disruption and its interest in land.

The local authority has refused to recognise the disruption to D Ltd's business on the basis that it is E Ltd who is the owner of the land. The relevant legislation permits the local authority to pay compensation to the owner of expropriated land for the 'value of the land expropriated' and the 'cost of disruption to the landowner's business'. Discuss.

Commentary

This is a problem-type question dealing with the issues relating to separate legal personality and the exceptions to it. The answer requires an application of the principles relating to the agency, piercing the corporate veil and the group enterprises arguments. A detailed knowledge of the leading cases such as the *Adams* v *Cape Industries plc* and the *DHN* case would be required.

Suggested Answer

The claims to be brought by the motorists would be first considered.

Claims by the Motorists

If there is to be any claim brought by the motorists it would be against D Ltd who had been involved in designing the automatic navigation system. However, the motorists would be concerned with the fact that the subsidiary only has a paid-up capital of £1,000. This would not be sufficient assets to meet all the claims. When judgments are obtained the plaintiffs in their actions would want to proceed against the assets of C plc. The first point to be made here is that, based on *Salomon v A. Salomon & Co. Ltd* [1897] AC 22, even if the subsidiary D Ltd is part of the group of companies headed by C plc, the large multinational, the company C plc is entitled to take advantage of the corporate structure to minimise its liabilities. It then has to be considered whether D Ltd could be treated as an agent of C plc.

Agency

D Ltd can be considered as an agent of C plc as, for all intents and purposes, the subsidiary carried out an aspect of C plc's business, that is, the manufacture of cars with the aim particularly of producing the automatic navigation system so as to ensure that it could be fitted into cars manufactured by C plc.

In *Re FG (Films) Ltd* [1953] 1 WLR 483, the court was concerned with a company incorporated in England to produce a film when in actual fact the expertise and the finance came from an American company whose chairman was also the majority shareholder of the British company. The involvement of the English company in the making of the film was found to be as agent of the American company. The only difficulty with reliance on *Re FG (Films) Ltd* is that it can be seen as being a case concerning a sham company as quite clearly the American company with the screening rights wanted the tax advantages which would have been available by having the film classified as British.

It would also be difficult to rely on the agency argument based on *Smith Stone & Knight Ltd v Birmingham Corporation* [1939] 4 All ER 116. This is the case as in Smith Stone, although the concern was with how the business of the subsidiary was being carried out, and the control which the parent had over the board of the subsidiary, the important difference is that the business that the parent company acquired was being effectively run by the parent with the subsidiary having no interest in the business assets.

The court in *Smith Stone & Knight* had found that the subsidiary had virtually operated like a department of the parent company in running the business acquired by the parent company. In our case D Ltd, even if its capital is only £1,000, is able to carry on a business from business premises even though these premises are not owned by D Ltd.

The next aspect that has to be considered is whether the incorporation of a subsidiary such as D Ltd to carry out what could turn out to be a dangerous project in the sense that there could be the potential for negligence actions in the event of something going wrong could be treated as a 'sham'.

Piercing the Corporate Veil

The plaintiffs bringing the claim against D Ltd may want to argue that C plc has incorporated D Ltd deliberately to avoid any liabilities that could arise out of the project going wrong. It is therefore necessary to consider the issue of a 'sham' company. *Jones* v *Lipman* [1962] 1 WLR 832 was specifically singled out in *Adams* v *Cape Industries plc* [1990] Ch 433 as an example of a sham. The court in *Jones* v *Lipman* had found that the company incorporated there was merely to avoid an order of specific performance and was a creation of Mr Lipman to achieve this. The court in *Adams* v *Cape Industries plc* case was of the view that the intention of the corporators was relevant in considering if the company was a sham. The court was of the view that Mr Lipman's motive for incorporating the company and transferring the land to the company was to avoid an order of specific performance. Here, although one might actually see C plc's motives of taking advantage of the corporate structure to the disadvantage of persons having a claim against D Ltd, that alone was not going to be recognised as being sufficient. The crucial factor is again whether D Ltd had its own business being carried out at the premises.

The other point to note here is that there is nothing on the facts to suggest that anyone had dealt directly with D Ltd thinking that it was C plc. In English law merely because a subsidiary may be under-capitalised in its business ventures would not be sufficient reason to pierce the corporate veil.

In the circumstances it could be said that the motorists who have got claims against D Ltd can only proceed against D Ltd for negligence and there would be no possibility of establishing any claim against C plc.

The question of whether D Ltd could also claim compensation for disruption to its business against the local authority would be considered next.

Claim against the Local Authority for Compensation in Relation to Business Disruption

The issue that has to be considered here is exactly which business is being carried on from the land and whose business has actually been disrupted as a result of compulsory acquisition.

It is possible to argue that the way in which C plc had organised its business was like a partnership involving the business of the various subsidiaries. That is, E Ltd, while owning the properties, was itself not carrying out its own business but actually helping to fund the business of D Ltd which in turn was carrying out the business of C plc. In this way one could interpret the business being disrupted as being the business of not E Ltd but the business of D Ltd which also is the business of C plc being carried out at these premises. One could also state here that we are concerned with the realities of the situation. In the *DHN* case such an approach was taken by the Court of Appeal. However, the *DHN* case was doubted in the later House of Lords' decision of *Woolfson* v *Strathclyde Regional Council* 1978 SC (HL) 90. The House of Lords in *Woolfson* did not think that the separate legal entitites of subsidiaries within a group can be easily disregarded unless there are 'special circumstances' indicating that the company is being used as a 'façade concealing true facts'.

The Court of Appeal in *Adams* v *Cape Industries plc* also doubted if the *DHN* decision could be used as an authority for any general proposition as referred to by Lord Denning of treating subsidiaries within a group as being one economic enterprise. However, the Court of Appeal in the *Adams* case was prepared to accept the decision of *DHN* as being correctly decided as a case concerning the interpretation of specific legislation.

This would mean that if the question of the business of the owner is arrived at purely on the interpretation of the particular legislation dealing with the compulsory acquisition then a court would be prepared to consider that possibility. On the approach of the interpretation of the particular language of the statute it may be argued by E Ltd that the economic reality was what legislation was concerned with when it referred to the business of the owner.

In *Revlon Inc.* v *Cripp & Lee Ltd* [1980] FSR 85, the question arose whether goods were 'connected in the course of trade with the proprietor of the trade mark' under section 4(3) of the 1938 Trade Marks Act. The proprietor of the trade mark was not Revlon Inc. (Revlon) but Revlon Suisse SA (Suisse). The court held that the goods traded by Revlon were connected with Suisse. The court was prepared to accept that from the economic point of view the mark was for the benefit of the Revlon group.

It could be argued here that when E Ltd owned the various premises in which the various subsidiaries carried on business the business of the owner would mean the business of the group. It could be argued that what is being achieved here is the treatment of various subsidiaries as being mutually dependent and it is that which would enable the conclusion that the business that is disrupted is not just E Ltd's business but also the business of the group.

It is submitted that despite the questioning of the correctness of the *DHN* case generally in the *Woolfson* case, the House of Lords in *Woolfson* did not find the mutual economic dependence in that particular case between Mr Woolfson and Solfred Holdings and the other company M & L Campbell Ltd.

3 The Doctrine of *Ultra Vires* and Agency

INTRODUCTION

The area of the doctrine of *ultra vires* has come under a great deal of reform since the 1989 Companies Act. A student should when considering the questions in this chapter consult the relevant chapters in the leading textbooks dealing with the reform of the *ultra vires* doctrine. It is the authors' view that for the purpose of examinations, it is not necessary to consider the special treatment by the 1989 Companies Act of charitable companies.

Students should realise that the main issues today are whether the reform introduced by the 1989 Companies Act after the Prentice Report serves shareholders well or whether the law has gone too far in protecting third parties. We would urge students to read Dr Frank Wooldridge's article 'Abolishing the *ultra vires* rule' (1989) 133 SJ 714. Dr Wooldridge provides some insights on what had taken place in the debates in the House of Lords, when the Companies Bill was considered.

There is also the issue of the first EC Directive on company law. References have been made to this in respect of the abolition of constructive notice in answers.

Students should also consider the Company Law Review Steering Group's consultation document entitled *Modern Company Law for a Competitive Economy: The Strategic Framework*. A summary of this document is set out in ch. 5 of *Cases and Materials on Company Law* by Andrew Hicks and S. H. Goo.

Students should aim to understand the organic theory whereby individual officers as well as the board of a company can be treated as a distinct organ of the company. For more details see ch. 8 of *Gower's Principles of Company Law*.

A good knowledge of this area in the course of any examination revision would also require some analysis of whether the UK Parliament has correctly implemented article 9 of the First Directive. This has been considered in the answers.

QUESTION 1

'The doctrine of *ultra vires* before the reforms brought in by the 1989 Companies Act was a nuisance to the company and a trap for the unwary third parties. The doctrine of *ultra vires* was of no value in terms of protection for members or creditors.' Discuss.

Commentary

The question requires an appraisal of the common law doctrine of *ultra vires* and how it came to be interpreted by the courts. You would then have to deal with the changes brought in by the 1989 Companies Act and consider its implications on the doctrine.

Suggested Answer

The term '*ultra vires*' as used in the question refers to the principle at common law that a company cannot enter into any transactions that have exceeded its objects clause. The House of Lords had decided in *Ashbury Railway Carriage and Iron Co. Ltd* v *Riche* (1875) LR 7 HL 653, that whenever a company, whether incorporated by or under a statute, acted beyond the company's objects clause in the memorandum then such acts were void as beyond the company's capacity even if ratified by all the members of the company.

When considering the House of Lords' decision in *Ashbury* one finds that it was particularly concerned with the protection of creditors so as to ensure that a company does not venture into some business which causes it to face a risk wholly different from anything that is inherent in the present business activities.

The years after the *Ashbury* decision found the advisers of companies circumventing the decision by drafting objects clauses that were wider than the models set out in the Tables of successive Companies Acts. The development also meant that the draftsman was including, besides the objects of a company, various powers that a company could exercise. In fact, shortly after the *Ashbury* case the House of Lords had decided in *Attorney-General* v *Great Eastern Railway Co.* (1880) 5 App Cas 473 that every reasonable power incidental to the main objects had to be implied. In the early part of the twentieth century the House of Lords in *Cotman* v *Brougham* [1918] AC 514 upheld the validity of another device commonly used by the draftsman of objects clauses that is a paragraph that would treat every paragraph of the objects clause as capable of standing as an independent object without it being ancillary to any main objects.

When we consider the case law we would find that very often companies proceed on with new lines of business and innocent parties later discover that they have no remedy against the company. In *Re Jon Beauforte Ltd* [1953] Ch 131, the company was by its objects clause empowered to carry on the business of costumiers, gown, robe, dress and mantle makers and tailors. The objects clause also contained the other usual clauses including that the directors should be able to carry on any other trade or business whatever which can, in the opinion of the directors, be advantageously carried on by the company in connection with or as ancillary to any of its main businesses.

The company, at some stage, was minded to carry on the business of manufacturing veneered panels which was *ultra vires*. The company had ordered a supply of fuel on its letterhead which showed it as being in the business of manufacturers of veneered panels. Although the third party argued that the fuel supplied could have been used for *intra vires* purposes such as heating offices, the court nevertheless held that the third party had constructive notice of the memorandum and the objects clause and was treated as being aware of the actual objects of the company together with actual notice of the company's business stated on the letterhead. It was held that the third party was deemed to have known that the company was in a business that was *ultra vires* and could not enforce the transaction.

It would be observed at this stage that the principle that the objects clause was in the memorandum and that the memorandum is a public document and so third parties had constructive notice, as it can be seen in *Re Jon Beauforte*, contributed to difficulties encountered by third parties.

Another development that had taken place was the move by the courts to attempt to restrict the scope of wide-ranging objects clauses by interpreting certain objects as being merely powers so as to be ancillary to main objects whatever the actual wording of the objects clause. In *Re Introductions Ltd* [1970] Ch 199, a company was by its objects clause empowered to organise exhibitions for the Festival of Britain. The company later proceeded to carry out pig farming which was a failure and the company was wound up. The liquidator resisted a claim by a charge holder when money was borrowed for the purposes of pig farming. The court here was concerned with the argument by the creditor that since the company's objects clause contained a *Cotman* v *Brougham* clause, the power to borrow money could stand as a separate and independent object.

The court rejected this argument. In the opinion of the court a purpose such as borrowing money cannot be capable of standing on its own as a separate object. It was held that at the time of borrowing the money must be borrowed for an object of the company and the particular purpose to which the money was going to be put was not an actual object of the company.

It is argued that this decision as to whether a particular object is capable of being an independent object is very arbitrary and one cannot help noticing that the court is really driven by policy considerations so as to ensure that a company does not turn certain powers such as borrowing money into substantive objectives. But the question is if the objects clause describes a purpose as an object a court should accept this. The decision in *Re Introductions* can be compared with the later decision of *Re Horsley and Weight Ltd* [1982] Ch 442, where the Court of Appeal held that the object of granting pensions to past and present employees and directors and their dependants was capable of being treated as a substantive object of the company. This was one of the cases where liquidators were trying to bring misfeasance proceedings against directors by alleging that certain transactions were *ultra vires*.

What was also happening at this stage was that the strict *ultra vires* doctrine, that is, the company's lack of capacity, was being confused with illegality arising from the directors' lack of authority. It was, one could say, an attempt by the courts to impose some check on the company's powers particularly as regards gratuitous acts. However, it was being achieved at the cost of making this area of law complex and it was also becoming evident that the *ultra vires* doctrine was no longer achieving its original purpose. Before the major reform of the *ultra vires* rule brought in by the 1989 Companies Act the House of Lords had come to clarify the position as regards objects and powers by stating that it was all a question of the construction of the objects clause and whether a particular paragraph was a power or object would be ultimately left to the court to be interpreted. The House of Lords also made it clear that so long as a company had acted within the objects clause, whether the transaction was in the interests of the company was a matter of directors' fiduciary duties.

Over the years it became plain that most companies would want to do business on the basis that they had full legal capacity like any ordinary individual. In fact Professor Prentice in his report, *Reform of the* ultra vires *rule: a consultative document*, had recommended that companies should be afforded the capacity to do any act whatsoever and should have the option of not stating their objects in their memorandum.

However, the changes introduced by the 1989 Companies Act took a different approach to what was recommended by the Prentice Report. The Companies Act 1989 retained the idea of an objects clause but companies can now introduce an objects clause by virtue of a new section 3A that was added to the 1985 Companies Act which provides for a company to carry on any business that a 'general commercial company' can carry on. The object of the new section 3A is to encourage the use of simple general statements of objects.

The other change that was introduced was that a new section 35 was introduced to the 1985 Companies Act whereby no act could be called into question either by the company or the third party dealing with the company on the basis that it exceeds the company's objects clause. In assessing the changes brought in by the 1989 Companies Act one could say that today the company or third parties need not be concerned with the issue of interpretation of the objects clause. Also the 1989 Companies Act brought about change by the abolition of the doctrine of constructive notice in relation to the memorandum and articles of association. At the time of writing, these provisions are not yet in force.

The new section 35 does preserve the directors' fiduciary duties in observing the limitations in the objects clause and the company can choose whether or not to ratify any breach of this fiduciary duty.

The new section 35 of the 1985 Companies Act does permit a member to restrain the company by injunction from acting *ultra vires*. However, this is now unlike the earlier common law, as section 35(2) only permits an injunction if the company is carrying out an *ultra vires* act which is not an act that the company is bound to carry out.

The subsection retains the protection for the individual shareholder. The law clearly has therefore proceeded to protect third parties and this certainly is an improvement over the earlier law.

In conclusion, one can state that the change in the law would reduce the need for litigation in this area and it would also mean that the courts would not have to make arbitrary distinctions in the interpretation of the objects clauses.

QUESTION 2

Does the Companies Act 1989 ensure (outside the area of transactions *ultra vires* the company) a company will not be able to escape liability for transactions entered into by its directors or employees?

Commentary

The question is concerned with the amendments brought in by the 1989 Companies Act whereby the new section 35A was added to the 1985 Companies Act. It would be necessary first to consider the changes brought in by section 35A to show whether it would achieve its aim of protecting third parties who dealt with companies.

Suggested Answer

The company being an artificial person can only act through its organs and agents. The English common law has always proceeded on the basis that authority to so act, like all aspects of agency, must be based on either actual authority, that is, the articles of association or memorandum actually conferring authority or what can be termed apparent or ostensible authority. In the Court of Appeal decision of *Freeman and Lockyer* v *Buckhurst Park Properties (Mangal) Ltd* [1964] 2 QB 480, Diplock LJ stated that 'actual' authority was a legal relationship between principal and agent created by consensual agreement to which they alone are parties. Its scope is to be ascertained by applying ordinary principles of construction of contracts including any express words used, usages of the trade or the course of business between the parties.

The most important limitation that exists as regards the actual authority of a director or any agent to whom the directors might delegate authority is what is set out in the articles of association. Ostensible authority is the authority of an agent as it would appear to third parties. Sometimes this is referred to as agency by estoppel whereby the principal is estopped from denying a representation even though the agent does not have actual authority.

The attitude of the common law in this area was also influenced by the fact that the investments of the members of a company should be protected by making everyone who dealt with a company responsible for seeing that restrictions implied by its constitution on the use of its assets were observed.

The principles in *Turquand*'s case (*Royal British Bank* v *Turquand* (1856) 6 E & B 327) ensure that since the articles and memorandum are documents that are registered, a third party dealing with a company should be entitled to assume that whatever is required to be carried out by the company has been complied with.

However, with the United Kingdom's membership of the European Community it became necessary for the United Kingdom to implement the First Company Law Directive. This required member States to ensure protection of third parties, so that grounds on which obligations are entered into in the name of the company are not invalid. Following the United Kingdom's first attempt to implement this in section 9 of the European Communities Act 1972, we now have sections 35A and 35B of the Companies Act 1985. Before considering the relevant sections in the Companies Act it would be useful to consider some of the key elements of art. 9(2) of the Directive. The Directive refers to the 'organs of the company', and also it refers to limits on the powers of the organs arising under the statutes or from a decision of the competent organs. When the UK Parliament legislated that the board of directors of a company was to be referred to in place of the organs, and 'statutes' referred to the articles of association. By the present section 35A a person is deemed as dealing in good faith when a company is a party to some transaction or act and such transaction is deemed free of any limitation under the company's constitution including limitations deriving (a) from a resolution of the company in general meeting or a meeting of any class of shareholders or (b) from any agreement between the members of the company or any class of shareholders. Leaving aside the need to reform this aspect of authority to deal on behalf of a company because of the reform of the *ultra vires* rule, it was also found that there were some difficulties in interpretation with the earlier version which first appeared as section 9(1) of the European Communities Act 1972 and later reproduced as section 35 of the 1985 Companies Act. In analysing the new section 35A one would have to start by considering the words 'the power of the board of directors to bind the company or authorise others to do so'. This would mean that whenever the board of directors of a company purport to exercise any powers in excess of the articles of association or memorandum or authorise others to do so the company cannot escape the consequences of the act. The purpose of the provision is to validate purported transactions and acts. However it may be argued that the section has no application if the persons acting as directors have not been properly appointed or the decision to authorise the transaction was carried out at a board meeting which was inquorate. In these circumstances any third party can only rely on the indoor management rule in *Turquand*'s case.

The next element to be considered is 'deals with' the company. Previously under section 9(1) of the European Communities Act and section 35 of the 1985 Companies Act the statute provided that it had to be a 'transaction decided on by the directors'. Section 35A(2)(a) now provides that a person 'deals with' a company if he is party to any transaction or other act to which the company is party to. This effectively now overrules the decision of Lawson J in *International Sales and Agencies Ltd* v *Marcus* [1982] 3 All ER 551. In that case cheques were drawn on the company's bank account by a director to pay off a debt incurred by a deceased fellow director. Clearly this was not a transaction with the company. Now, however, section 35A refers to an act to which the company is a party and can cover situations where the company carries out acts where no consideration is provided by the other party.

The next element to be considered is 'dealing with a company in good faith'. Again section 35A (2)(b) effectively overrules Lawson J in *International Sales and Agencies Ltd* v *Marcus* [1982] 3 All ER 551. Section 35A(2)(b) provides that 'a person shall not be regarded as acting in bad faith by reason only of his knowing that an act is beyond the powers of the directors under the company's constitution'. In *International Sales*, Lawson J proceeded on the basis that if a third party had knowledge of a breach of fiduciary duties on the part of a director then not only would the third party be treated as a constructive trustee but also that he would not be dealing in good faith. On the earlier authorities dealing with good faith the *obiter dictum* of Nourse J concerning the earlier section 35 would still be relevant when his lordship had stated that '. . . a person deals in good faith if he acts genuinely and honestly in the circumstances of the case'. The view of Nourse J in *Barclays Bank Ltd* v *TOSG Trust Fund Ltd* [1984] BCLC 1, was that to show that someone acted in good faith it is not necessary to show that the person acted reasonably.

It is still uncertain what could constitute bad faith. One possibility here is that if the third party and a director of a company deliberately acted so as to cause a loss to the company and had acted fraudulently this could be treated as acting in bad faith. The new section 35A does assist the third party by providing that there is a presumption of a third party having acting in good faith and placing the burden on the company to rebut that presumption.

The new section 35A, like the new section 35 in relation to the reform of *ultra vires*, proceeds on the basis of directors observing the limitations imposed by the company's articles internally. Therefore section 35A(4) permits a member to bring an action for restraining the company acting inconsistently with any restrictions imposed by the articles. However, this would be lost if the company is already bound to carry out the act. The directors can still be in breach of their fiduciary duties and any action must be brought against them either by the company or through a derivative action.

Section 35B on the other hand protects third parties by ensuring that they are not bound to enquire as to whether the company is permitted by the memorandum or of any limitations on the powers of the company. It is also necessary to note here that the section only refers to transactions and not to acts. What is not certain is whether this would mean that gratuitous acts, which cannot come within the meaning of 'transactions', are covered by the section.

In assessing the new section 35A it must be observed that the original Directive by art. 9 did not permit a third party to rely on a transaction as binding if he had actual knowledge that the organs did not have the necessary authority. The Directive was thus more concerned with what in English law would be treated as constructive notice and to prevent a third party from having notice merely because the document is a registered one. The English version of the Directive, now section 35A, would certainly do away with the need to invoke the doctrine of constructive notice which was harsh on third parties. However, what we have now with the new section 35A are difficulties with the imposition of constructive trusts (see generally on this Hanbury and Martin, *Modern Equity*, 14th ed., ch. 12).

In the case of *Re Montagu's Settlement Trusts* [1987] Ch 264, Megarry V-C referred to the necessary knowledge to impose a constructive trust which according to him is either knowing of a breach of fiduciary duties at the time of receipt of property or shutting one's eyes to what is obvious in relation to a breach of fiduciary duties.

It could be said that although with section 35A and section 35B third parties dealing with a company would be better protected in most cases, without having to rely on the rule in *Turquand*'s case or any doctrine of ostensible authority, there still remain the uncertainties of the interpretation of the elements of section 35A considered above and the problems of constructive trusts.

QUESTION 3

A Ltd is a company incorporated with the following objects clause: 'to manufacture, promote and market health foods and nutrition supplements'. The company objects clause contains also the following paragraphs, that is, 'the directors are authorised to carry out any business which in their opinion could be carried out effectively with the company's main objects'. There is also a clause providing that each subclause shall be construed as an independent object and not merely as subsidiary to objects mentioned in other subclauses. The objects clause also permits the company to borrow and to lend and advance money, to give credit to such firms or companies or persons on such terms as may be expedient. A Ltd, with increasing competition in the health food business, decides to go into the business of offering acupuncture treatment. In pursuance of this it purchases premises to set up an acupuncture centre. Also to help acquire the necessary state-of-the-art equipment it borrows a sum of £50,000 from B bank plc. A Ltd is now consulting a firm of public relations consultants on an exclusive advertising campaign to promote its acupuncture business. Tim, a minority shareholder, is concerned that the venture by the company would lead to a failure that could affect the reputation of A Ltd. Advise Tim of his legal position. Would your advice be different if the board of directors of A Ltd had just considered the possibility of acquiring land to set up an acupuncture centre but have not entered into any agreement to purchase.

Commentary

In dealing with the question you want to examine each of the acts of the company in turn to deal with the issue of *ultra vires*. It is necessary here to develop the present law in respect of *ultra vires* on how it still operates internally. The answer would also have to consider the rights of the member in respect of *ultra vires* transactions and the remedy that may or may not be available. The question does also involve aspects of directors' fiduciary duties to be covered in a subsequent chapter. Good organisation of an answer is as important if not more important than the substantive law material to be covered in the question.

Suggested Answer

Taking the issue of the purchase of the land for the purposes of setting up an acupuncture centre, the question that has to be considered is whether the purchase of land for the purposes of acupuncture is *ultra vires*.

The objects clause of A Ltd identifies its main objects as the manufacture, promoting and marketing of health foods. In the circumstances any purchase of land for the purposes of the business must involve that main object. Thus it would be possible to state that the purchase purely for the purposes of an acupuncture centre would be exceeding the objects clause.

However, the next question that has to be considered is whether the directors could rely on the paragraph that permits the company to carry out any business which in the opinion of the directors can be carried out effectively with the company's main objects. This type of clause was first considered by the Court of Appeal in *Bell Houses Ltd* v *City Wall Properties Ltd* [1966] 2 QB 656. The

Court of Appeal here held that the company could rely on such a clause so long as the directors honestly believed that the particular business could be carried on advantageously in connection with or as an ancillary to the company's main business.

However it must be observed that in the *Bell Houses* case the court had found that the particular business, that is, of introducing financiers for a building project was related to the company's main object of acting as developers of housing estates. The Court of Appeal had also viewed the particular transaction in *Bell Houses* as one which had come to the company by accident. This was the case as Bell Houses itself had obtained an opportunity to receive the finance but could not use it as it had no developments at that time. As a result when the plaintiffs had indicated that they were interested in financing to be obtained Bell Houses decided to introduce its source to the plaintiffs for a commission.

In our situation the setting up of an acupuncture centre would appear to be a totally new business whatever the directors may think about its effects on the existing health food business.

Danckwerts LJ in the *Bell Houses* case had been able to distinguish cases on which Bell Houses was attempting to rely on to argue that the transaction was *ultra vires* by stating that the cases referred to were instances where there was a complete departure from the real objects for which the company was set up.

It could be on the other hand argued by the company that the clause leaves the decision as to what business could be effectively carried out with the main objects as a matter purely for the directors and the test is a subjective test. In fact the Court of Appeal in *Bell Houses* agreed that it is the directors who should be left with the final decision, as the articles and memorandum constitute the basis on which the shareholders participate in the business of the company. On balance it may be said that the only possibility of the purchase of land being *ultra vires* is if we proceed on the basis that the acupuncture business is a totally new business. Next we would have to consider Tim's rights, if any, in respect of the transaction being *ultra vires*.

Effects of the Transaction Being Ultra Vires

The new section 35 of the Companies Act 1985 introduced by the 1989 Companies Act provides that no act by the company can be questioned on the basis that it was outside the objects clause.

This would mean that the *ultra vires* doctrine has no application externally. However, the new section 35 does maintain the need for directors to be bound by their fiduciary duties to observe limitations in the objects clause and the member still has his personal rights preserved by section 35(2) of the Act, which would permit a member to bring proceedings to restrain the doing of an *ultra vires* act.

Proceeding on the basis that the board has already made a decision and the company has entered into the transaction to purchase the land, the remedy of an injunction would not be available.

The present section 35(2) would not permit the bringing of the action if the company is fulfilling an obligation arising from a previous act of the company.

As for any breaches of fiduciary duties on the part of the board of directors, this would be a matter for the company to pursue as a cause of action. No individual member would have a right to pursue a remedy in respect of this.

Turning now to the other part of the question asking whether it would make any difference if the board is considering the acquisition of land for the purposes of an acupuncture centre.

At this stage Tim as a member can apply for an injunction to restrain the company acting *ultra vires*. This is the case as there is no possibility of the company showing that it is carrying out some act that it is bound to perform by virtue of an earlier legal obligation.

Turning now to the bank loan of £50,000 to acquire the site for the acupuncture centre. Is the borrowing of £50,000 from B Bank plc *ultra vires*?

The directors of A Ltd would want to rely on the clause in the objects clause that would permit them to borrow money by arguing that since each clause is capable of standing as a separate object, the borrowing of money should be interpreted as such. However, in *Re Introductions Ltd* [1970] Ch 199, the Court of Appeal was concerned with a company that granted debentures as security for a loan. The company had power to borrow money and it was held that this was not an independent object. In the judgment of Harman LJ, 'borrowing is not an end in itself and must be for some purpose of the company'.

Re Introductions Ltd was followed in *Rolled Steel Products (Holdings) Ltd* v *British Steel Corporation* [1986] Ch 246. The courts in this area have come to some arbitrary decisions. In *Re Horsley and Weight Ltd* [1982] Ch 442, the Court of Appeal proceeded on the basis that, since there was a clause providing for each clause of the objects to be treated as a separate object this should be given effect. In *Re Horsley* the Court of Appeal held that the power of a company not only to provide pensions to employees and ex-employees but also to provide funds in the assistance or promotion of any charitable or public purpose could stand as a substantive object.

It is argued that in view of *Re Introductions* it would be difficult to argue that the borrowing of money could itself be treated as an independent object. It must also be further noted that in *Re Horsley* the issue before the court was the taking out of a pension policy for the benefit of a former director which could be said to be incidental to the main objects of the company.

Consequences of the Transaction Being Ultra Vires

As set out earlier, in view of the new section 35 of the Companies Act 1985, the bank, being a third party, would be able to enforce the loan if the transaction has been entered into. Tim as a shareholder cannot bring a personal action as, by section 35(2), an injunction would not be available once the company has entered into the transaction.

The next issue to be considered is the use of the money for the purposes of acquiring the equipment for the acupuncture business and the public relations campaign.

Tim's Rights in Relation to the Use of the £50,000

By section 35(2) the member would not be able to bring proceedings if the company is carrying out 'an act to be done in fulfilment of a legal obligation arising from a previous act'. It is therefore necessary always to consider what is the previous act of the company. If the company is only still negotiating with the public relations firm then it would not be bound by any previous act. The same approach would also apply to the proposed purchase of the equipment. As such if the company has entered into any contract to take delivery of the equipment then the company would be bound by that previous act.

Tim as a minority shareholder should also be advised that by section 35(3) the company can in general meeting ratify any *ultra vires* transaction by special resolution. The possibility of ratification would now reverse the decision of *Ashbury Railway Carriage and Iron Co. Ltd* v *Riche* (1874) LR 7 HL 653, where the House of Lords had held that an *ultra vires* transaction was not ratifiable.

4 Articles of Association and the Section 14 Statutory Contract

INTRODUCTION

The current section 14 of the 1985 Companies Act is an important part of company law as it emphasises the extent of members' rights. The main issue here has always been whether a member can rely on the statutory nature of the contract to enforce what may be essentially outsider rights, that is, enforcement of rights in other capacities such as a company solicitor, or director. In this area students should aim to be aware of the different academic interpretation of the scope of the present section 14 and to what extent outsider rights are enforceable. Consider here the Law Commission's Report No. 246 entitled *Shareholder Remedies*. An extract is set out in ch. 6 of *Cases and Materials on Company Law* by Andrew Hicks and S. H. Goo.

On the distribution of powers between the different organs of the company, the effects of regulation 70 of Table A of the 1985 Companies Act should be considered. In the course of the answers this aspect has been considered in the light of the decision in *Breckland Group Holdings Ltd* v *London & Suffolk Properties Ltd* [1989] BCLC 100.

Alteration of Articles

With the introduction of what is now section 459 of the Companies Act 1985 it would be possible to envisage shareholders relying on the unfair prejudice remedy whenever there is any 'fraud on the minority' as opposed to challenging it under the common law. However exam questions at times get candidates to deal with advice to the parties on the basis of the common law excluding the consideration of any statutory remedies.

In the circumstances it would be necessary to pay careful attention to the cases on the 'fraud on the minority' tests, including the cases on expropriation of shares where you should aim to contrast *Brown* v *British Abrasive Wheel Co. Ltd* [1919] 1 Ch 290, with *Sidebottom* v *Kershaw, Leese & Co. Ltd* [1920] 1 Ch 154. These matters are elaborated in the answers that follow.

QUESTION 1

Explain the doctrine that the articles of association are a form of contract between the members and the company as a separate legal entity and between the members themselves. Should there be reform of the present wording of section 14 of the Companies Act 1985?

Commentary

This is an essay question on the nature of the section 14 contract. You should explain the doctrine as referred to in the question, deal with the case of *Hickman v Kent or Romney Marsh Sheep-Breeders' Association* [1915] 1 Ch 881, and then the other leading cases. After that you should consider academic commentaries on the section 14 contract.

Suggested Answer

The doctrine referred to in the question has its origins in judicial decisions starting from the case of *Hickman v Kent or Romney Marsh Sheep-Breeders' Association* [1915] 1 Ch 881. In that case the Association, which was a registered company, maintained a register of a particular breed of sheep which the Association was concerned with. A dispute broke out between Mr Hickman and the company which took steps to remove his sheep from the register thus making them less valuable. The articles of association of the company required any disputes between the company and any member to be referred to arbitration. However, Mr Hickman commenced proceedings and applied for an injunction to prevent the association expelling him. The company in turn decided to apply for a stay of Mr Hickman's action by relying on the statutory provisions relating to arbitration by arguing that the relevant provision in the articles constituted 'a written agreement to submit present or future differences to arbitration'.

In his judgment Astbury J held as regards what is now section 14 of the Companies Act 1985 that the memorandum and articles of a company constitute a contract between the company and its members '*qua* members'. Therefore Mr Hickman was bound by the terms of the articles and had to refer the dispute to arbitration. Decisions following the *Hickman* case had to deal with the interpretation of Astbury J's decision on the scope of the section 14 contract.

In *Beattie* v *E. & F. Beattie Ltd* [1938] Ch 708, the articles of E. & F. Beattie Ltd required any dispute between the company and a member to be referred to arbitration. A director, who was also a member of the company, applied for a stay of the proceedings against him on the basis that the provision in the articles was a written agreement to submit to arbitration. The dispute here concerned him in his capacity as a director and the Court of Appeal refused the stay on the basis that the article was a contract that was in relation to members' rights and not in respect of what can be termed as 'outsider rights.'

However, in the House of Lords decision in *Quin & Axtens Ltd* v *Salmon* [1909] AC 442, a director was able to enforce a provision in the articles giving him a veto as a managing director. Professor Lord Wedderburn in an article in the *Cambridge Law Journal* in 1957 at p. 194 argued that a member suing '*qua member*' could enforce provisions of the articles even if it conferred rights in the capacity of an outsider and cites the decision in *Quin & Axtens* as authority. The position taken by Professor Lord Wedderburn is that the enforcement of the right by Salmon was a contractual right. Professor Lord Wedderburn states that all provisions of the articles are contractual and not just those relating to membership rights. (For a review of the controversies in this area see R.R. Drury, 'The relative nature of a shareholder's right to enforce the company contract' [1986] CLJ 219).

The proposition put forward by Lord Wedderburn has not been without criticism. G.N. Prentice in 'The enforcement of "outsider rights"' (1980) 1 Co. Law 179 takes the view that not every provision of the articles is contractual and only those provisions that are necessary for the relevant organs of the company to function can be treated as having a contractual effect.

The next aspect to be considered here is the function of the articles as a contract between the company's members. This aspect is sometimes referred to as the articles being a form of a 'social contract'. This view is from the speech of Lord Cairns in *Eley* v *Positive Government Security Life Assurance Co. Ltd* (1876) 1 ExD 88, where his lordship referred to the articles of association as stating the arrangement between the members. They are an agreement *inter socios*.

All this has been interpreted to mean that when it comes to enforcement of the provisions it has to take place through the company since no member has between himself and another member any right beyond that which the contract with the company gives. However in *Rayfield* v *Hands* [1960] Ch 1, a member of a company whose articles provided that a member who intended to transfer his shares had to inform the directors of the company who would take the shares equally between them at a fair value was able to enforce the article against the directors on the basis that they were a class of members. The judge, Vaisey J, had, however, indicated that the conclusion he was arriving at would not be of general application. His lordship had concluded that the private company in that case was more of a partnership.

From the above discussion it would be apparent that the courts would in such cases as *Beattie* v *E. & F. Beattie Ltd* treat directors as being 'outsiders.' All this is not very satisfactory as quite clearly directors should be treated as insiders since they owe fiduciary duties to the company and are also obliged to comply with provisions of the articles and memorandum.

If an outsider, that is, a person who is to be conferred rights such as a company's solicitor or a director, purports to rely on the articles of association, then such a provision would not be contractual but merely a direction or authorisation. This would be the case even if the outsider becomes a member of the company. In *Eley* v *Positive Government Security Life Assurance Co. Ltd* (1876) 1 ExD 88, Mr Eley, the company's solicitor, attempted to rely on a provision in the company's articles enabling him to be a solicitor of the company for life and could only be removed for misconduct. Eley had become a member after a year of the company's incorporation. The court held that the action could not succeed. It would appear that Mr Eley together with other members could have prevented the company acting in breach of the articles but Mr Eley himself could not. However, in the *Eley* case the court considered it contrary to public policy for members to prevent the company appointing anyone else as a solicitor.

On the question whether the present section 14 of the Companies Act 1985 should be reworded, from the above discussion it would be more sensible to modify the wording so that it not only refers to the members and the company, but also for the contract to refer to directors and other officers of the company. However, the Law Commission in its Report (No. 246, *Shareholder Remedies*) concluded that there is no need to reform section 14 of the Companies Act 1985. The main reason being that most interested parties in the response felt that the section 459 remedy was very much wider than a personal action.

QUESTION 2

The shares of Adventurers Ltd, a company dealing in computer games, are mainly held by Lingle and MacClean. The articles appointed them and one other person, Richardson, as directors. The articles also appointed Lingle and

MacClean as managing directors. The articles are in the form of Table A of the 1985 Companies (Tables A to F) Regulations. Article 70 provided that 'the managing directors, the said Lingle and MacClean' could veto any board decision relating to investment in excess of £500,000. Because of differences of opinion between Lingle and the other directors, Lingle exercised his veto. The other directors then proceeded to call a general meeting where they resolved to proceed with the decision to invest the £500,000. Advise Lingle.

Commentary

The question requires a consideration of the enforceability of 'outsider rights' in respect of the statutory contract created by section 14 of the Companies Act 1985. The other issue that requires consideration is the validity of the ordinary resolution passed by the majority shareholders and whether this would permit the majority to ratify and prevent the director from bringing an action.

Suggested Answer

Enforcement of the Provisions of the Articles

The articles of association would constitute a statutory contract by virtue of section 14 of the Companies Act 1985. Lingle could argue here that since the articles are to have contractual effect he should be able to obtain an injunction as a shareholder to restrain the company from acting on the resolution. Lingle could rely on the decision in *Quin & Axtens Ltd* v *Salmon* [1909] AC 442.

However, in *Hickman* v *Kent or Romney Marsh Sheep-Breeders' Association* [1915] 1 Ch 881, Astbury J interpreted the earlier provision similar to section 14 as only permitting membership rights to be enforced. In *Quin & Axtens* the plaintiff was proceeding with an application for an injunction to enforce an 'outsider' right, that is, other than in a capacity as a shareholder. This appears to be inconsistent with *Beattie* v *E. & F. Beattie Ltd* [1938] Ch 708, where Mr Beattie had not been able to enforce a provision of the articles to have a matter submitted to arbitration. Following the reasoning in the *Hickman* case the court in *Beattie* had held that for the purposes of obtaining a stay under the Arbitration Act the reference of the dispute to arbitration must arise from the contract between the company and member in his capacity as a member. One could distinguish the cases by arguing that the member, if he wanted to enforce the articles such as in *Beattie* should have sought an injunction restraining the court proceedings brought by the company, by asserting his membership rights. *Quin & Axtens* thus could be distinguished on the basis that the managing director in that case had succeeded as he had sued to obtain an injunction so as to have the affairs of the company conducted in accordance with the articles. Now to deal with the powers of the general meeting to ratify the breach of the articles.

The general meeting being the ultimate organ of the company can ratify any breaches of the articles. The principle is a very old one that in any association there is an obligation to settle disputes within the association by majority decisions. Lord Wilberforce had said in *Re Kong Thai Sawmill (Miri) Sdn Bhd* [1978] 2 MLJ 227, that 'Those who take interests in companies limited by shares have to accept majority rule'. However, the majority rule which is part of the rule in *Foss* v *Harbottle* (1843) 2 Hare 461, is subject to exceptions. In *Edwards* v *Halliwell* [1950] 2 All ER 1064, Jenkins LJ identified the personal rights as one of the exceptions. To his lordship, where personal rights of membership have been violated, then these are matters which are not regarded as questions of internal management.

The issue here is whether the right to enforce the particular provisions of the articles can be treated as an enforcement of a 'personal right'. In *Edwards* v *Halliwell* the defendant trade union amended its rules to increase the membership contribution without the two-thirds majority by ballot which was required by its constitution.

The Court of Appeal in the *Edwards* case went on to conclude that whilst a company is the proper plaintiff whenever the alleged wrong is done to a company or an association of persons, there was another rule noted by Romer J in *Cotter* v *National Union of Seamen* [1929] 2 Ch 58. This rule, which was affirmed by the Court of Appeal in *Edwards* was that if what a member is complaining of is a matter that is beyond the power of a simple majority, that is, it requires a special majority, then a member should be able to sue. The rationale for this as affirmed by the Court of Appeal in *Edwards* is that if a member has no remedy then it would permit a company to act in breach of its articles. Thus in *Edwards* the member was able to maintain a personal action against the defendant union.

On our facts it could be argued on behalf of Lingle that what the majority are attempting to do is virtually to rewrite the articles, without going through the procedure laid down in the Companies Act 1985 relating to the alteration of articles.

The other point that can be also considered here is that in the *Edwards* case, Jenkins LJ also went on to state that the trade union rules were rules that relate to the membership rights and that any invasion of such rights should result in a member being able to sue. The problem in our case here is that the particular provision, that is, the veto right which Lingle is going to be concerned with, cannot be termed a 'membership right' shared by all the other members.

In conclusion, Lingle would be able to proceed to apply for an injunction restraining the company from acting on the resolution passed by the general meeting. The majority shareholders cannot in these circumstances argue that as an ultimate organ they should be able to decide whether the breach should be ratified. It could also be argued here that, whatever position a court may take on the issue of personal rights in terms of enforcing the provision of the articles, Lingle's strongest argument here is that the majority cannot now interfere by passing an ordinary resolution with the right of veto which treats the directors who could exercise this right as being a separate and distinct organ with certain management functions. In the circumstances even if the general meeting by an ordinary resolution can remove directors what cannot be done is to interfere with a business judgment, which is subject to a veto power.

QUESTION 3

N Co. Ltd is a company where 49 per cent of the shares are held by A Co. Ltd and the other 51 per cent of the shares are held by B Co. Ltd. B Co. Ltd has instructed solicitors to commence proceedings against the managing director of N Co. Ltd who is a majority shareholder in A Co. Ltd. The directors of N Co. Ltd have not met to decide on the institution of legal proceedings. Directors of A Co. Ltd are concerned with the action that has now been commenced by B Co. Ltd. They are also concerned with the move now by B Co. Ltd to call a meeting of the shareholders to ratify the bringing of proceedings in the name of N Co. Ltd. Discuss.

Commentary

The question requires consideration of the general meeting's residuary power in relation to the use of the company's name in litigation. There is also a need to consider the decision of *Breckland Group Holdings Ltd* v *London & Suffolk Properties Ltd* [1989] BCLC 100.

Suggested Answer

The first point that has to be considered here is the effect of the articles of association on registration. A Co. Ltd would want to proceed on the basis that art. 70 of Table A would constitute a contract between the company and its members whereby the company's business has to be managed by the board of directors.

In support of the proposition A Co. Ltd could rely on the decision in the House of Lords in *Quin & Axtens Ltd* v *Salmon* [1909] AC 442. The House of Lords approved the Court of Appeal's decision permitting a member to bring a personal action to ensure that the company's affairs are conducted in accordance with the company's articles. A Co. Ltd would therefore want to seek an injunction to restrain N Co. Ltd from acting on any resolution to be passed and also to obtain a declaration that the proper organ to institute legal proceedings in the name of N Co. Ltd is the board of directors.

However, A Co. Ltd would also be concerned with the issue of which organ can exercise authority to ratify litigation commenced without the authority of the directors.

Power to Litigate

It may be argued by B Co. Ltd that, although by art. 70 the powers of management are delegated to the board of directors, members should be able to control the members of the board as directors are their delegates and not just the company's officers. In *Isle of Wight Railway Co.* v *Tahourdin* (1884) 25 ChD 320, the court refused the directors of a statutory company an injunction to restrain the holding of a general meeting one purpose of which was to appoint a committee to reorganise the management. The Court of Appeal held that it was a serious thing to prevent shareholders from holding a meeting of the company when such a meeting is the only way in which they can interfere if the majority of them think that the course taken by the directors is not for the benefit of the company.

The other point that has to be considered here is that the board has not yet made any decision one way or another and at the moment the action has been commenced without authority of the company. Later cases after the *Tahourdin* case have proceeded on considering the wording of what was at one time art. 80 of Table A of the 1948 Companies Act. In *Gramophone & Typewriter Ltd* v *Stanley* [1908] 2 KB 89, the Court of Appeal had held that even though art.

80 permitted the general power of management to be subject to 'such regulations as may be prescribed by the company in general meeting', this was not sufficient to enable the general meeting to give directions to the board, on the basis that directors are not servants to obey directions given by the shareholders as individuals as they are not agents appointed by and bound to serve the shareholders as their principals. More recently in *Breckland Group Holdings Ltd* v *London & Suffolk Properties Ltd* [1989] BCLC 100, the court was confronted with a situation like the present situation. There, Breckland Group Holdings Ltd owned 49 per cent and Crompton Enterprises Ltd owned 51 per cent of the shares of London & Suffolk Properties Ltd. There was also a shareholders' agreement which provided that the institution of legal proceedings by London & Suffolk had to have the support of one Crompton and one Breckland director. The shareholders' agreement also had provided for the appointment of one director on behalf of Breckland and two on behalf of Crompton.

An action was commenced without prior board resolution against the managing director of London & Suffolk Properties. The action was commenced by Crompton. Breckland sought an injunction to restrain Crompton from continuing with the action. The court held that since the company's articles of association adopted art. 80 of Table A of the Companies Act 1948 the jurisdiction to conduct the business of the company was vested in the board of directors and the shareholders in general meeting could not intervene to adopt unauthorised proceedings.

In his judgment Harman J also pointed out that the shareholders' agreement had pointed in the direction of shareholders having agreed to leave the matter of litigation to the board and that had to be respected. It is submitted that despite the views of Harman J that art. 80 confides the management of the business to the directors and the majority of shareholders could not interfere, the position in the *Breckland* case was that there was yet no decision at the level of the board when the litigation was started. In *Danish Mercantile Co. Ltd* v *Beaumont* [1951] Ch 680 it was held that the company in general meeting could ratify litigation that was commenced without authority. The position it is submitted would have applied in the *Breckland* case if it were not for the influence of the shareholders' agreement which specifically provided for the decision of the board to be taken on 'material litigation'.

Further, Harman J was also aware of the shareholders' agreement restricting the freedom of shareholders' action. In our case here since A Co. Ltd and B Co. Ltd do not have a shareholders' agreement along the lines of the *Breckland* case the position could be distinguished.

The Effect of Article 70 of Table A 1985

Although art. 70 permits the general meeting to give directions by special resolution on the exercise of the company's powers, it could be argued that on the facts of the question there is no issue of any special directions being given on the exercise of the company's powers but rather the ratification of an act that was commenced without the authority of the board.

Conclusion

Given the decision of the Chancery Division in *Breckland Group Holdings*, there would be a great possibility of a court on our facts concluding that since the company is incorporated on the basis of art. 70 of Table A 1985, the instituting of litigation is a power of the company delegated to the board and, as stated in the *Quin & Axtens Ltd* v *Salmon* decision preferred in *Breckland*, the general meeting can only intervene by altering the articles.

QUESTION 4

X Ltd, 'the company', has a share capital of £60,000 in £1 shares which are held as to 15,000 shares by John, 12,500 each by Jim, James and Jason. John, Jim, James and Jason are all directors. The rest of the shares are distributed among five different shareholders.

John has expertise in the area of the retail trade in relation to costume jewellery. When they first incorporated the company, Jim, James and Jason had approached John to acquire his business. As part of the agreement under which John's business was acquired the company's articles incorporated the following clause: 'No resolution by the board of directors of the company, or by the company itself, which concerns the acquisition of any business in excess of £50,000 shall be valid unless agreed to by any shareholder holding more than 20 per cent of the issued share capital of the company'.

Jim, James and Jason are now interested in acquiring a ladies' dressmaking business which is being sold by the owner for £70,000. The three of them are of the view that the company should expand its business. The other five different shareholders who take no active part in the business will vote the way James would want them to vote. John is concerned with the possible alteration of the articles to remove his veto power. He is also concerned with any other means that could be employed to have his veto eliminated.

Commentary

The question requires the consideration of the test relating to the challenge to any alteration to remove the veto in favour of John. On the issue of what other means can be employed to remove the veto, it is necessary to consider the possible expropriation of his shares. For the purposes of the question you would have to consider the possibility of John relying on section 459 of the Companies Act 1985.

Suggested Answer

John's first concern would be with the possibility of the other three directors taking steps to alter the articles.

Alteration of Articles

The articles of association will have to be altered in accordance with section 9(1) of the Companies Act 1985. The other directors would be able to obtain the majority that is required to pass the special resolution which is three-quarters of the votes. See section 378 of the Companies Act 1985. A company's power to alter the articles is also restricted by the need to exercise the company's power to alter its articles bona fide for the benefit of the company as a whole.

In the leading Court of Appeal decision of *Allen* v *Gold Reefs of West Africa Ltd* [1900] 1 Ch 656, Lindley MR stated that the power of alteration must be subject to the requirements of law and equity which govern the exercise of powers. It is here that the Court of Appeal made reference to 'bona fide for the benefit of the company as a whole'. The next issue here is to consider what is meant by this.

The Court of Appeal in *Greenhalgh* v *Arderne Cinemas Ltd* [1951] Ch 286 held that the phrase 'the company as a whole' does not mean 'the company as a commercial entity, distinct from the corporators,' but rather 'the corporators as a general body'.

Lord Evershed in the *Greenhalgh* case went on to state that the court has to consider the position of the 'individual hypothetical member' and consider whether what is proposed is, in the honest opinion of those who voted in favour, for the hypothetical person's benefit. X Ltd could argue here that removing the particular provision in the articles could deal with an increase in business competition by diversifying the company's business. X Ltd then can argue that if we were to consider the position of the 'hypothetical member' who could represent any present or future shareholders, the amendment of the articles to remove John's veto would be for the benefit of that member.

John should also be advised that a company cannot effectively be prevented from altering its articles as the right of alteration is conferred by statute in what is today section 9 of the Companies Act 1985. In fact one of the consequences of the articles of association forming part of the statutory contract caused by section 14 of the Companies Act 1985 is the power of the company to alter the articles. In the *Greenhalgh* case Lord Evershed stated that a special resolution to alter the articles would not be allowed if it discriminated between the majority shareholders and the minority shareholders, so as to give the former an advantage of which the latter were deprived.

In the *Greenhalgh* case the alterations took away from the minority the right to acquire other members' shares if those other members could secure an ordinary resolution approving a transfer to an outsider. However, to the Court of Appeal the ability of the 'hypothetical member' to transfer his shares more freely was said to be in the interests of the company.

On our facts here it could be said that removing the veto would only affect John's position as member and would discriminate against him as a minority shareholder. In the Australian decision of *Australian Fixed Trusts Pty Ltd* v *Clyde Industries Ltd* [1959] SR (NSW) 33, the directors of Clyde Industries Ltd proposed to alter the articles so as to make it virtually impossible for votes to be cast in relation to shares held on behalf of unit trusts. Having discovered no 'corporate purpose' for the alteration the court relied on the test of discrimination. It was held that the proposed alteration was invalid as it reduced the voting power of specific shareholders and thus increased the voting power of the other shareholders. One can on the other hand argue that X Ltd has here a 'company purpose' in deciding that the clause has to be removed in view of John's possible objections to diversifying the business.

Possible Acquisition of John's Shares by the Company

The company may also want to alter the articles so as to enable the company or directors after giving notice to have John's shares acquired at a fair price. This would ensure that the company would be able to eliminate John as a shareholder and prevent him from exercising the veto power under the articles.

It could be said that such an alteration has to be shown to be bona fide in the interests of the company, when members vote on it.

In *Brown* v *British Abrasive Wheel Co. Ltd* [1919] 1 Ch 290, a resolution expropriating the shares of the minority was treated as purely benefiting the majority and not the company. In the *Brown* case the company was in need of capital with shareholders holding 98 per cent of the shares not willing to put up the capital unless they could acquire the 2 per cent held by the minority shareholders. The minority failed to sell and the company altered the articles so as to make the minority shareholders transfer the shares upon request in writing of the holders of 90 per cent of the shares. The court found that the majority had acted in good faith when wanting to appropriate the shares of the minority in the interests of the company, but the court still permitted an injunction restraining the company from passing the resolution. The court was of the opinion that a clause like this would have been valid if it had been in the articles at the time of incorporation. Then a minority shareholder would have become a member on the basis of such a provision and would not be able to complain if his shares were expropriated. But the court was not prepared to accept the insertion of such a clause in the articles purely in the interests of the majority as opposed to the company. In the case of X Ltd here, even if the majority are honestly of the view that John's continued participation in the company as a shareholder would not be in the company's long-term interests, any provision enabling expropriation of his shares could be challenged as a fraud on the minority.

However, in the later Court of Appeal decision of *Sidebottom* v *Kershaw, Leese & Co. Ltd* [1920] 1 Ch 154, the Court of Appeal did permit a company to alter its articles to permit appropriation of the minority shareholders' shares. The *Sidebottom* case was distinguished on the basis that the acquisition of the shares of any shareholder competing with the company, which was a director-controlled company, was in the interests of the company.

It can be argued that any question of whether the expropriation of John's shares is in the interests of the company is an objective question for the court to decide taking into account all the circumstances, including whether the shares are being acquired at a fair value. It could be also argued on behalf of John that the reason for the provision in the articles was to ensure that John had a say in the long-term interests of X Ltd after it had acquired his business and that his expectation would have to be taken into account by the majority when voting on any resolution to alter the articles.

John could also rely on the judgment of Foster J in *Clemens* v *Clemens Bros Ltd* [1976] 2 All ER 268. Although the decision does not directly deal with any issues of alteration of articles it would be relevant in relation to the exercise of the majority's voting power in the general meeting. The case concerned a private company where the plaintiff held 45 per cent of the shares and her aunt was a director (unlike the plaintiff) and held 55 per cent of the shares. Resolutions were passed at a general meeting by the aunt's votes to issue further shares to the other directors and to trustees of an employees' share-ownership scheme. All this would effectively deprive the plaintiff of negative control through her power to block a special resolution and would reduce the value of her pre-emptive rights under the articles, if another shareholder wanted to sell.

Foster J here when considering the position of the hypothetical member substituted the actual minority shareholder to consider if it was for the benefit of the minority shareholder. In our case, any expropriation and for that matter any removal of the veto power in the articles would not be for John's benefit.

For the completeness of the answer we would have to mention the availability of section 459 of the Companies Act 1985 . As indicated earlier, you should always read a question carefully as you may not be required to consider the statutory remedy.

Section 459 Petition

The removal of the veto or the expropriation of John's shares could be treated as acts on the part of the company that are 'unfairly prejudicial' to the interests of John as a member. This aspect is covered in chapter 6 dealing with section 459 of the Companies Act 1985 more specifically.

5   The Rule in *Foss* v *Harbottle*

INTRODUCTION

One of the things that everyone remembers from the study of company law besides *Salomon*'s case is the so-called rule in *Foss* v *Harbottle*. However, very often students are unable to offer a statement of the rule and to be able then to apply the rule or elaborate further on its consequences. We would therefore in the introduction of this chapter offer possibilities in terms of how the rule could be stated. It must be remembered here that it is an area where a great deal of academic controversy has developed and different textbooks offer slightly different statements of the rule.

We would in the course of this chapter refer to a statement of the rule based on the seminal articles by Professor Lord Wedderburn entitled "Shareholders' rights and the rule in *Foss* v *Harbottle*' [1957] CLJ 194, [1958] CLJ 93. To Professor Lord Wedderburn the rule in *Foss* v *Harbottle* is made up of two limbs. First the corporate rule limb and secondly the majority rule limb. In the opinion of *Mayson, French and Ryan on Company Law*, the rule is expounded from the speech of Lord Davey in *Burland* v *Earle* [1902] AC 83, PC, and expressed as follows. First if a wrong is done to a company (as a person separate from its members) then only the company may sue for redress. This is expressed by Mayson, French and Ryan as the 'proper plaintiff' principle. Secondly the court would not interfere with the 'internal management' of companies acting within their powers. This is referred to by Mayson, French and Ryan as the 'internal management' principle. The internal management principle, they also state, contains the 'proper plaintiff aspect', which is that if there is a question of internal management of a company a court would not be prepared in any proceedings to have such a matter determined except in proceedings brought by the company itself. Thirdly, a member cannot sue to rectify a mere informality or irregularity if the act when done regularly would be within the powers of the company. In our view the corporate rule limb emphasises that the company is a separate legal entity and that any irregularity, so long as it is not an infringement of a member's personal right, is only actionable by the company. This would cover what is termed in the opinion of Mayson, French and Ryan as being the 'proper plaintiff principle'. As for what we would call the majority rule limb, it encompasses both the 'internal management' principle and the 'irregularity' principle set out by Mayson, French and Ryan.

When dealing with a problem-type question, our advice is that you should decide whether an act of the company, be it in general meeting or by the board of directors, infringes a personal right. If on the other hand the wrong involves a wrong done to the company or a breach of a provision of the articles, the next step to consider is whether the majority of shareholders could ratify the wrongdoing. It is at this stage that you would be able to decide if the shareholder should be the proper plaintiff.

If the wrongdoing is ratifiable then the individual shareholder cannot bring an action. On the other hand, if the wrongdoing is not ratifiable then even if the company is the proper plaintiff a member of the company can bring what is termed a derivative action so long as the requirements are satisfied. This will be dealt with in the course of the answers in this chapter.

This brings us to the very practical consequence of the rule in *Foss* v *Harbottle* and that is whether a shareholder is to bring a personal action when there is an infringement of a personal right. Here you should consider what is understood as a personal right. You should look at the material covered in chapter 4 of this book on the 'section 14 contract'.

If a derivative action is the only possibility then you should be in a position to consider the two important cases which show the type of obstacles a minority shareholder is to overcome. These cases are the Court of Appeal decision in *Prudential Assurance Co. Ltd* v *Newman Industries Ltd (No. 2)* [1982] Ch 204 and the judgment of Knox J in *Smith* v *Croft (No. 2)* [1988] Ch 114.

In our view a practical approach to the rule in *Foss* v *Harbottle* would mean that the topic should not be approached from the point of the rule and the so-called exceptions to the rule, rather the best way to appreciate the consequences of the rule in *Foss* v *Harbottle* is to appreciate the distinctions between a personal and a derivative action. Students should now consider the Law Commission's Report on shareholder remedies (No. 246, *Shareholder Remedies*). An extract is set out in ch. 13 of *Cases and Materials on Company Law* by Andrew Hicks and S. H. Goo.

QUESTION 1

'It is an elementary principle that A cannot, as a general rule bring an action against B to recover damages or secure other relief against B on behalf of C for an injury done by B to C. C is the proper plaintiff because C is the party injured, and therefore, the person in whom the cause of action is vested. This is sometimes referred to as the rule in *Foss* v *Harbottle* (1843) 2 Hare 461.' Discuss.

Commentary

The question requires the discussion of what can be termed the proper plaintiff principle. It would be useful here to start by referring to the *Foss* v *Harbottle* decision itself and set out what can be termed an exception to the proper plaintiff principle. It would also be necessary to deal with the attitude of the Court of Appeal in *Prudential Assurance Co. Ltd* v *Newman Industries Ltd (No. 2)* [1982] Ch 204, where the quotation for the question comes from.

Answer

The passage above is an expression of the rationale behind what can be termed as the rule in *Foss* v *Harbottle* (1843) 2 Hare 461. The decision proceeds on the basis that since legal rights of a company belong to the company, the company being a separate legal entity, this is not a cause of action that belongs to the members, and members do not have any legal standing to bring any action on behalf of the company.

In *Foss* v *Harbottle* two members of the company had suspected that various persons including some directors of the company had made secret profits as promoters of the company. The two members then commenced an action against the alleged wrongdoers 'on behalf of themselves and all other proprietors of shares except the defendants'. Wigram V-C said, 'It was not, nor could it successfully be, argued that it was a matter of course for any individual members of a corporation thus to assume to themselves the right of suing in the name of the corporation. In law the corporation and the aggregate members of the corporation are not the same thing for purposes like this.' The company on incorporation acts by its organs, namely, the board of directors and in some cases the general meeting. On the issue of whether the company should commence any litigation, the decision would have to be taken by the organ which, under the company's constitution, has authority to institute legal proceedings. By Table A art. 70 it would be the board of directors.

A question that could be posed here on the interpretation of the articles of association is whether it would be practical to leave the board of directors to decide on the issue of commencing corporate litigation against directors for breach of their duties. It would be seen that the matter should be left to the general meeting. However, the decision of *Breckland Group Holdings Ltd* v *London & Suffolk Properties Ltd* [1989] BCLC 100, would suggest that the question of commencing proceedings should be treated as being determined by the articles, namely, in Table A, art. 70. It must be noted that the proper plaintiff principle would be followed here even if the majority of members were to support the action by a member. This was held to be the case in *Mozley* v *Alston* (1847) 41 ER 833. Here certain directors had refused to retire from the board as required under the articles and retained the company's seal which was the property of the company. The Lord Chancellor had treated the wrongdoing as being a wrong done to the company and treated the company as the proper plaintiff.

It is now necessary to consider the situations in which the courts have been prepared to create exceptions to the proper plaintiff rule. The starting-point on the so-called exceptions would be the judgment of Jenkins LJ in *Edwards* v *Halliwell* [1950] 2 All ER 1064. It is necessary to observe that his Lordship was concerned with two types of exceptions in formulating his so-called exceptions which are:

(a)   Situations where a derivative action would be permitted by the courts. Here there is a dispute between the member of a company who is normally a minority shareholder and those in control over the company's litigation and there is no applicaton under section 459 of the Companies Act 1985.

(b)   Situations which really do not come within the scope of the rule in *Foss* v *Harbottle* since the issue raised would not be treated as a matter of internal management, and so the company is not required to be the plaintiff.

The exceptions are:

(a)   *Ultra vires* acts. It must be noted that with the new section 35(3) of the Companies Act 1985 the general meeting can ratify by a special resolution *ultra vires* acts unless the member is able to show a fraud on the minority.

(b)   Special majorities. If a matter could only be sanctioned by a special majority, then a member could sue if only a simple majority attempted to sanction the matter.

(c) Personal rights. If the personal and individual rights of membership have been invaded then the rule in *Foss* v *Harbottle* has no application.

(d) Fraud on the minority. This is probably the only real exception to the rule in *Foss* v *Harbottle*, as the minority shareholder or shareholders are allowed to bring what is known as a derivative action on the basis of fraud and control on the part of wrongdoers.

It would be necessary now to consider the issue of fraud. In *Burland* v *Earle* [1902] AC 83, the Privy Council held that the term 'fraud' would cover acts which involve the majority endeavouring directly or indirectly to appropriate to themselves money, property or advantages which belong to the company, or in which the other shareholders are entitled to participate.

There has always been controversy over exactly what is meant by 'act of a fraudulent character'. In the judgment of Megarry V-C in *Estmanco (Kilner House) Ltd* v *Greater London Council* [1982] 1 WLR 2, 'fraud' in the context of 'fraud on the minority' was wider than fraud at common law and would cover 'fraud' on a power when voting takes place in the general meeting.

Further Vinelott J in *Prudential Assurance Co. Ltd* v *Newman Industries Ltd* [1981] Ch 257, having surveyed the cases, had gone on to state that 'fraud on the minority' could cover not only cases where directors misappropriate the company's property but also cases where directors are in breach of their duty to the company to exercise proper care and not obtain a benefit for themselves.

It can be argued that the approach of Megarry V-C in *Estmanco (Kilner House) Ltd* v *Greater London Council* is consistent with the authorities and it may be explained on the basis of the unusual facts of the case as the Greater London Council was a majority shareholder with voting rights which was clearly voting to discontinue an action on behalf of the company that was directed to injure a voteless minority.

The Court of Appeal in *Prudential Assurance Co. Ltd* v *Newman Industries Ltd (No: 2)* [1982] Ch 204, did not consider the extensive survey of the rule in *Foss* v *Harbottle* by Vinelott J as it had found that on the evidence before the court there was no fraud. As for the element of control that has to be established, in the *Prudential Assurance* case the Court of Appeal was of the view that control can cover a wide spectrum from the wrongdoers being in absolute control to a situation where control can be established not only on the votes of the delinquent directors but also other shareholders over whom there is influence or who are apathetic. Turning now to deal with the issue of the so-called personal rights exception, if a member is wronged in his capacity as a shareholder, such as where dividends declared are not paid or votes cast at a meeting are ignored, these would involve personal rights. The personal right does not exist if there is a loss in value of shares arising from damage done to the company.

In the *Prudential Assurance* decision the Court of Appeal stated that when a shareholder acquires a share he accepts the fact that the value of his investment follows the fortunes of the company, and the shareholder can only ensure that the company observes the limitations of its memorandum of association and the other shareholders observe the limitations imposed on them by the articles. The Court of Appeal also went further to state that if a shareholder attends a meeting convened by directors on the basis of a fraudulent circular he will have a right to claim his travelling expenses and the expense of attending the meeting. However, the shareholder cannot recover for the dimunution of the value of his shares through any loss suffered by the company.

In some circumstances when a person causes loss to a company there may also be an existing relationship between the person and a company either in contract or tort which is breached by the loss caused to the company. In *George Fischer (Great Britain) Ltd* v *Multi-Construction Ltd* [1995] 1 BCLC 260 a contract made by a parent company had been breached by the other party who had to pay damages for that breach. Since the parent company was a party to the contract the parent company was the only proper plaintiff. The parent company was able to sue for loss in value of its shares in the subsidiaries, which was due to the damages caused by the breach of contract.

QUESTION 2

Venture Ltd ('the company') is a company whose main objects are property development and the leasing of residential and commercial property. The company's articles are in the form of Table A. The share capital is made up of £500,000 of ordinary shares of which £300,000 is held by Jack and Jill (who are directors of the company) with the remaining shares held by various investors including £5,000 by Jones a retired schoolteacher. The other remaining shareholders are business associates of Jack and Jill who vote as instructed by Jack and Jill. It has now come to light that in 1999 when the company was pursuing negotiations to purchase a number of old houses in a certain part of north London, Jack and Jill purchased one of the houses for themselves jointly which they have now sold for a handsome profit to an investor from Hong Kong who was interested in old English houses. It has also further come to light that a piece of land that the company had in general meeting resolved to sell in 1999 to Jack and Jill was sold at a gross undervalue and Jack and Jill have now sold to other developers at some 10 times the price they paid. Jones is now concerned with bringing proceedings against Jack and Jill to recover the secret profits in relation to the purchase and resale of the property in North London. Jones is also concerned with the sale of the company's land to Jack and Jill at an undervalue, as he believes there was a loss to his shareholding. Advise Jones.

Commentary

The answer would have to identify the type of cause of action that Jones would be concerned with; that is, whether there is any basis for a personal action or a derivative action. If the derivative action has to be pursued then the answer would have to deal with the elements of 'fraud' and 'control'. Finally there is also a need to consider section 320 of the 1985 Companies Act and its relationship with the 'fraud on the minority' exception.

Suggested Answer

It would be important to observe first that the two matters that Jones is going to be concerned with involve wrongdoings that are wrongs done to the company. In *Prudential Assurance Co. Ltd* v *Newman Industries Ltd (No. 2)* [1982] Ch 204, the Court of Appeal held that the shareholders only had a right to vote at meetings and to participate in the company's affairs as permitted by the articles of association. Even if as a shareholder Jones might argue that a sale of the asset of a company at an undervalue could have an effect on his shareholding, in law the loss would be treated as one suffered by the company.

If the company is the proper plaintiff, then based on *Foss* v *Harbottle* the majority of shareholders should be able to decide if there has been any wrongdoing such as breach of fiduciary duties and whether any action should be brought against the wrongdoers.

Taking first the issue of secret profit from the sale of the property at North London, Jack and Jill having purchased the property for their benefit.

Jack and Jill are directors of the company and by acting in that capacity while pursuing the negotiations have profited from their position as fiduciaries. This obligation is the traditional overriding equitable obligation established in the

House of Lords decision of *Bray* v *Ford* [1896] AC 44, that it is an inflexible rule of equity that a person in a fiduciary position is not unless otherwise expressly provided to make a profit or to put himself in a position where his interest would conflict with his duty. Based on our facts it would not be difficult to establish a breach of the fiduciary duties of Jack and Jill. What has to be considered is whether the majority of shareholders including Jack and Jill could use their votes to approve what has been done.

Fraud on the Minority by Those in Control

The Privy Council in *Burland* v *Earle* [1902] AC 83 explained the meaning of 'fraud on the minority' as covering acts of a fraudulent class or beyond the powers of the company and also where the relief is sought against those who control the shares which are voted to have the wrongdoing ratified.

In *Menier* v *Hooper's Telegraph Works* (1874) LR 9 Ch App 350, the majority shareholder in a company had contracted to make and lay a submarine telegraph cable for the company. At a later stage the majority shareholder had decided that another person should have the contract. The majority shareholder then caused the company to abandon the contract. A minority shareholder was permitted to pursue a derivative action to recover for the company from the majority shareholder the profits made from the diverted contract.

The Privy Council decision of *Burland* v *Earle* would suggest that so long as a director is selling to his company property that he did not acquire when acting in his capacity as a director the transaction could be ratified and it would not be treated as fraudulent.

The difficulty in our case here is that the company was also pursuing the opportunity to purchase the old houses in north London, and so they could be, following the Privy Council decision of *Cook* v *Deeks* [1916] 1 AC 554, property that belongs in equity to the company. In these circumstances when Jack and Jill make any profits it will not merely be a matter of incidental profits. In that event it would be possible to treat Jack and Jill's conduct in relation to the purchase of the property at north London as not being ratifiable and would be treated as 'fraudulent'.

Before dealing with any procedural aspects the next point that would have to be considered is the breach of fiduciary duties when the company's property was sold at a gross undervalue.

Sale of Company's Land to Jack and Jill

As a preliminary point it has to be noted that with section 320 of the Companies Act 1985 it is possible for a director to have an interest in a substantial property transaction with a company.

The facts do not indicate whether the value of the property brings the transaction within section 320. But assuming that the property is of the value to qualify as a substantial property transaction the company has followed the correct procedure of approving the transaction at general meeting.

Section 320 of the Companies Act 1985 also does not impose any restrictions on the director himself making use of his votes at the resolution in general meeting.

However, what would be of concern to Jones here is the gross undervaluation of the property which would tend to suggest gross negligence on the part of the directors. It could be assumed here that the directors have not exercised the skill that is necessary taking into account their knowledge and experience. The main issue that has to be considered here is whether there is a 'fraud on the minority' when the only wrongdoing is gross negligence.

In *Daniels* v *Daniels* [1978] Ch 406, a husband and wife were directors and majority shareholders of a company. The company sold to the wife for £4,250 some land which was sold by the wife for some £120,000. Although there was no intention to defraud the minority shareholders the court held that a derivative action would be permitted. The court proceeded on the basis that even if there was no fraud, if directors use their powers intentionally or unintentionally or negligently in a manner which benefits themselves at the expense of the minority, that can constitute 'fraud on the minority'.

On this reasoning it could be said here that Jack and Jill have benefited with the sale of the property at a profit after the sale to themselves at an undervalue. Turning now to the procedural aspects relating to Jones's claim.

The Derivative Action

In order to use the name of the company in proceedings against the directors, Jack and Jill, Jones would have to satisfy the court that there was 'fraud' and that there is wrongdoer control.

Jones would be able to establish here that even without the votes of the other shareholders, the wrongdoers have an absolute control of the votes. This would establish that the only way a claim can be brought is through a derivative action. We cannot state here that there is an independent organ to make the decision whether proceedings are going to be in the interest of the company.

QUESTION 3

Child Play Ltd (the company) has a share capital of £100,000 of ordinary shares divided amongst five shareholders as follows: Tom 10,000 shares, Dick 20,000 shares, Harry 30,000 shares, Georgina 10,000 shares and James 30,000 shares. The articles are on the basis of Table A 1985. All five shareholders were appointed as directors under the articles.

For some years there have been differences of opinion between the directors. James had always wanted to remove Tom as he felt that a relationship between Tom and Georgina was detrimental to the business as the two of them were involved in their personal relationship and hardly attended board meetings. James decides to call a general meeting of the shareholders, where a resolution is passed removing Tom as a director. Tom now seeks your advice in seeking an injunction to restrain the company from acting on the resolution as James did not convene a proper board meeting. Although a notice of the board meeting was sent out as required by the articles, the only person who had attended the meeting was James.

Commentary

The question examines the issue of irregularities within the company and the irregularity principle of the rule in *Foss* v *Harbottle*. The question requires consideration of the leading cases in this area starting with *MacDougall* v *Gardiner* (1875) 1 ChD 13.

Suggested Answer

First Tom has to be advised that even if he is the aggrieved party the conducting of meetings and any question of irregularity is a matter for the company to pursue. What can be termed as the internal management principle can be summarised as follows: the court would not interfere with the internal management of a company acting within its powers.

As part of the internal management principle it has also been held that the court would not be involved in any questions of irregularity unless the proceedings have been brought by the company itself.

The only way in which a member would be able to bring any proceedings is either if what has been infringed is a personal right of the member or alternatively the majority decisions are fraudulent or oppressive.

What has to be considered next is the Court of Appeal decision of *MacDougall* v *Gardiner* (1875) 1 ChD 13, which is often treated as the decision where the internal management principle has its origins.

The Internal Management Principle

In the *MacDougall* case a Colonel Gardiner had chaired a meeting of members of a company. The colonel would move for an adjournment whenever he was not happy with a resolution that was about to be passed. Colonel Gardiner also was aware that he would be able to obtain a vote on the adjournment by a show of hands but not on a poll. A member had demanded a poll which was refused by the colonel. The member together with other dissatisfied members brought an action based on the colonel's breach of the articles.

The Court of Appeal gave two reasons for dismissing the action of the members. First on a procedural aspect the court held that it could only provide a remedy if a substantive remedy is claimed as opposed to the determination of a question of law.

Secondly, the Court of Appeal considered the dispute about the holding of a poll to be a matter of internal management and the only plaintiff should be the company.

The Court of Appeal here was affirming the principle in *Foss* v *Harbottle* that nothing connected with the internal management is to be the subject-matter of an action unless the action is brought by the company. The Court of Appeal only recognised exceptions if the company has carried out an act *ultra vires* or the majority had acted in a manner that was oppressive or fraudulent.

What has to be examined next is the nature of the irregularity here when the resolution was passed by the general meeting to remove Tom as a director.

Removal of Tom as a Director

By section 303 of the Companies Act 1985 a company can remove a director by an ordinary resolution notwithstanding anything in its articles or any agreement between the company and the director.

The majority that would be required for an ordinary resolution would be a simple majority since the Companies Act 1985 does not define an ordinary resolution.

Tom's main concern would be with the failure of James to hold a valid board meeting. James's decision by himself to call for the extraordinary general meeting to remove Tom as director would be in breach of the articles as any board meeting to be valid must have at least two directors present. As such the instructions from James to call the meeting of shareholders would be invalid.

However, if the irregularity is the non-compliance with the article on the holding of the directors' meeting then if the court is satisfied that the end result of the resolution would have been the same even if the same procedure was followed the court would then not allow a member's action.

In the Court of Appeal decision of *Browne* v *La Trinidad* (1887) 37 ChD 1, there was a purported meeting of directors of La Trinidad at which it was resolved to call an extraordinary general meeting of the members. The Court of Appeal had found that although the meeting of the directors was invalid it was not prepared to question the decision taken to remove Mr Browne as a director at the general meeting. The Court of Appeal here reasoned on the basis that Mr. Browne had time to call another meeting of the directors and argue his point of view. Also the decision by the members at the general meeting was unanimous. Therefore it would not make any difference to the outcome of the matter even if the proper procedure was followed when the board of directors met.

A more recent application of the principle in *Browne* v *La Trinidad* is the judgment of Plowman J in *Bentley-Stevens* v *Jones* [1974] 1 WLR 638. The defendant company was a wholly owned subsidiary of another company. The plaintiff was one of the directors of the subsidiary. The board of the defendant company called an extraordinary general meeting to remove the plaintiff. The board of directors purported to serve notice of the extraordinary general meeting, but the board had not properly met in accordance with the articles. Following the passing of the ordinary resolution, the plaintiff proceeded to seek an injunction to restrain the defendant company from acting on the resolution. Plowman J denied the injunction on the basis that the application for the injunction came within the principle in *Browne* v *La Trinidad* where the Court of Appeal had stated that a court would not want to rule upon the company's adherence to strict rules where the irregularity could be set right at any moment. The Court was not prepared to accept the argument that the proceedings before the general meeting were a nullity because there was no properly convened board meeting.

It would therefore not be possible for Tom to argue that the proceedings in the general meeting were a nullity. Although in a case such as *Bentley-Stevens* the voting at the general meeting was unanimous and there was no doubt about the outcome of the meeting, on the present facts it could be said that if the majority of shareholders would vote in favour of removing Tom then it would not have made a difference in the outcome whether there was a properly convened board meeting.

QUESTION 4

Critically assess the proposition that both *Prudential Assurance Co. Ltd* v *Newman Industries Ltd (No. 2)* and *Smith* v *Croft (No. 2)* [1988] Ch 114 have reduced the rights of minority shareholders.

Commentary

The question requires the consideration of the interpretation of the 'fraud on the minority' exception to the rule in *Foss* v *Harbottle* and how the two cases referred to in the question have made it more difficult for minority shareholders in bringing derivative actions. This area of the law is quite important in problem-type questions where a conflict could arise where the company is challenging the minority shareholder's right to bring a derivative action.

Suggested Answer

The Court of Appeal in *Prudential Assurance Co. Ltd* v *Newman Industries Ltd (No. 2)* [1982] Ch 204 reviewed the requirements to be satisfied in the bringing of a derivative action. The Court of Appeal stated that any plaintiff seeking to bring a derivative action should be able to establish:

   (a)   that the company is entitled to the relief claimed and

(b)   that the situation can come within the exception to the proper plaintiff principle. This would mean that not only must 'fraud' be established but also that there is wrongdoer control. The Court of Appeal stated that control could be either actual legal control, that is, where the wrongdoers have absolute control or could be established if other shareholders may have voted with the wrongdoers even if those shareholders were not in any way involved with any wrongdoing.

The Court of Appeal made it clear that it would not be practicable to retain an 'interest of justice' exception. The view of the Court of Appeal in *Prudential Assurance* is that whenever the wrong is one that has been done to the company then it is for the appropriate organ of the company to decide if proceedings are to be brought. The Court of Appeal was particularly concerned with costly actions being brought by a minority shareholder with the company being liable for the costs. The Court of Appeal was clear in *Prudential Assurance* that the only way in which any action by a minority shareholder could avoid the procedural obstacles set out above is when the member is able to bring a personal action. The Court of Appeal was not prepared to accept in *Prudential Assurance* that any wrong done to a company can have an effect on a member's interest.

Turning to the decision of *Smith* v *Croft (No. 2)* here the main shareholders of a company were the defendants and they held shares carrying 62.5 per cent of the voting rights. The plaintiffs together with other shareholders held 14.44 per cent of the voting shares. The following allegations were made by the plaintiffs:

(a)   that the directors paid themselves excessive remuneration,

(b)   that the payments made to associated companies were an *ultra vires* gift,

(c)   that the payments made to the associated companies were in breach of what is now section 151 of the Companies Act 1985.

By the time the matter came before Knox J on an application to have the action struck out it was clear that the only viable claim that the minority shareholders could bring was one relating to the breach of section 151 relating to the providing of financial assistance towards the purchase of the company's own shares.

The company's argument here was that any act for recovery of property as regards the illegality in the breach of section 151 of the 1985 Companies Act was a course of action for the company to pursue and the plaintiffs' action should be struck out as not disclosing any reasonable cause of action.

Knox J relied on the test in *Prudential Assurance* and posed the question whether the plaintiff is being prevented improperly from bringing the proceedings on behalf of the company.

If it is an expression of the corporate will of the company by an appropriate independent organ that is preventing the plaintiff from prosecuting the action then the decision would be valid. On the facts the court found that the views of the other independent shareholders not involved in the dispute should have a say as to whether the derivative action should continue. The test that was proposed by Knox J in assessing the vote of the independent majority was to see whether the voting would be bona fide in the interest of the company.

The idea of looking for independent shareholders does raise the following problems. The test from *Allen* v *Gold Reefs of West Africa Ltd* [1900] 1 Ch 656 has to be considered and the court would have to consider if there was any risk of votes being cast in favour of the wrongdoers as opposed to voting in the interest of the company.

The other difficulty here is why the views of the independent shareholders have to be considered at the stage of the bringing of the derivative action when it had not featured at the stage of ascertaining if there was a fraud.

The wrongdoers can exercise control over the independent shareholders by persuading them not to bring a derivative action, when either a wrongdoing is not ratified or is not ratifiable.

At first instance in *Prudential Assurance*, Vinelott J took the view that when considering whether there was a fraud independent shareholders' views would have to be considered. To Vinelott J all acts are ratifiable by an independent majority. The Court of Appeal rejected Vinelott J's views and proceeded along the traditional basis by concentrating on the nature of the transaction when dealing with whether there is fraud. It may be said that the minority shareholder's position now has been made more difficult as there is a third limb to be considered besides considering fraud and control.

Deciding what is bona fide in the interest of the company would have some subjective elements and would allow the majority yet another opportunity to avoid defending any derivative action claim. Possibly in some cases, where appropriate, a minority shareholder would be better off proceeding by way of a petition under section 459 of the Companies Act 1985.

6 Statutory Remedies — Section 459 of the Companies Act 1985 and Section 122(1)(g) of the Insolvency Act 1986

INTRODUCTION

In dealing with the issue of corporate maladministration, that is, to deal with secret profits being made by directors at the expense of the company, minority shareholders have faced considerable difficulties with the rule in *Foss* v *Harbottle*.

There is also the problem of breaches of the articles and conduct of the company's affairs which disregard the minority shareholder's position. In recent years since the present version of section 459 of the Companies Act was introduced more minority shareholders have used a petition under section 459 as opposed to attempts to find exceptions to the rule in *Foss* v *Harbottle*.

In practical terms one would come across most minority shareholders being advised to use section 459 of the Companies Act 1985 in establishing that the company has acted in a manner that is unfairly prejudicial to the interest of the member. However, examination questions today often expressly state that you have to advise leaving out any statutory remedies. This would mean that a section 459 remedy should not be considered unless the question does not expressly exclude consideration of it.

As for the statutory remedy of petitioning that it is just and equitable that the company be wound up, again in practice often minority shareholders utilise this as an alternative to their petition under section 459. The winding-up petition would allege that the company is a type of 'quasi-partnership' where the exercise of legal rights within a company shall be subject to equitable considerations.

What you should be specifically concerned with here are the facts of a question to ensure that there is indeed a 'quasi-partnership' so to speak based on *Ebrahimi* v *Westbourne Galleries Ltd* [1973] AC 360. Again examination questions in this area can require answers to exclude any consideration of section 122(1)(g).

The winding-up remedy is a drastic one, and often it is utilised to put pressure on the majority shareholders to purchase the minority's shares. Such a remedy would be essentially a section 459 remedy and it is for this reason that in most cases petitioning shareholders put in a prayer for the winding up on the just and equitable ground.

Students should also consider the Law Commission's Consultation Paper No. 142 entitled *Shareholder Remedies*. The Law Commission proposes that there be a simple special procedure for cases where the principal complaint is of exclusion from management in a 'quasi-partnership' company. Further there is a recommendation that Table A include a provision entitling a minority shareholder exit rights. That is, to be able to demand to be bought out by other members at fair valuation in certain circumstances, such as on being dismissed from a directorship.

The Law Commission also wants to encourage alternative dispute resolution by including an agreement in Table A that disputes between the company and any member or between any members about any act or omission of the company must be referred to arbitration.

Students should also give consideration to the issue of whether the section 459 remedy should replace derivative actions and if there is a need for reform of the derivative action procedure.

QUESTION 1

Consider if the remedy in section 459 of the 1985 Companies Act has been overused. Are the courts interfering too much with the commercial decisions of companies?

Commentary

This question requires initially a description of the statutory remedy in section 459 of the 1985 Companies Act. The question also requires a discussion of the case law including now the first House of Lords decision on section 459 namely, *O'Neill* v *Phillips* [1999] 1 WLR 1092. The answer should mention the Law Commission's Report No. 246 on *Shareholder Remedies*.

Suggested Answer

The provisions in section 459 to 461 of the Companies Act 1985 was originally enacted as section 75 of the Companies Act 1980. The court can now provide a remedy if the affairs of a company were being conducted in a manner which is 'unfairly prejudicial to the interests of its members generally or some part of its members (including at least himself)'.

It must be noted from the onset that Parliament had introduced section 75 of the 1980 Companies Act to replace section 210 of the 1948 Companies Act as it was felt that the previous requirement that a petitioner establish that the affairs of the company were conducted in a manner that was 'oppressive' was too limited. Further, under the old law a petitioner has to not only establish that the affairs of the company were conducted in a manner that was oppressive but also that the circumstances of the case were such that the company be wound up on the ground that it was just and equitable to do so.

The change in the law has definitely seen more petitions now being presented under section 459 of the Companies Act 1985. Petitioners have also in their petitions dealt with the entire history of a company in great detail to establish an overall picture of prejudice and then this has been followed by extensive evidence and cross-examination. To a certain extent therefore it would appear that the remedy is overused. What would be considered next are some of the leading cases to ascertain if the courts have indeed intervened too much in the commercial decisions of companies.

To start with in *Re Sam Weller and Sons Ltd* [1990] Ch 682 the court held that the term 'interests' of the company is much wider than the term 'rights' and that members may have different interests even if their rights as members are the same. In the *Sam Weller* case the issue was whether the sole director who had conducted the affairs of the company for the benefit of himself and his family had conducted the affairs of the company in a manner that is unfairly prejudicial.

The court was prepared to question the company's directors relating to capital expenditure and concluded that inadequate dividends declared to the share-holders was unfairly prejudicial as the minority shareholders depended solely on the dividends for their income unlike the majority shareholder. The court rejected the argument that since the dividends were paid to all members holding shares, inadequate dividends could never be unfairly prejudicial as it affected all the members. In *Sam Weller* we see the court taking a broad approach by proceeding on the basis that Parliament by using the word 'interests' included something wider than 'rights'.

In *Re BSB Holdings Ltd No. 2* [1996] 1 BCLC 155, it was held that 'unfair prejudice' is not necessarily limited to cases of breach of fiduciary duty or the company's articles of association or any other relevant agreements or the provisions of the Companies Act. Again in *Re BSB Holdings* the court was prepared to consider the wording of section 459 and conclude that the wording of the section is wider and general. This point is significant as if one considers the earlier decision of *Re Saul D. Harrison and Sons plc* [1995] 1 BCLC 14, it may appear that only breach of directors' duties can give rise to a remedy under section 459. In *Re Saul D. Harrison*, Hoffmann LJ had concluded that the very minimum required to make out a case of unfairness is that the powers of management have been used for an 'unlawful purpose or the articles otherwise infringed'.

The development in *Re BSB Holdings* is interesting as certainly under the old section 210 of the 1948 Companies Act when dealing with 'conduct that is oppressive', a court would more likely to have provided a remedy if there was some serious breach of the provisions of the articles of association or a breach of fiduciary duties. The next point that has to be considered is how far the courts would proceed under the present section 459 when dealing with 'interests' of the members. In *Re Saul D. Harrison* Hoffman LJ, as he was then, adopted Lord Wilberforce's approach in *Ebrahimi Westbourne Galleries Ltd* [1973] AC 360 and stated that the personal relationship between a shareholder and those who control the company can invoke a 'legitimate expectation'. Lord Wilberforce had referred to this as being 'expectations', 'obligations' that are not necessarily submerged in the company structure. A good example of this is found in *Ebrahimi* itself where there was an undertaking on the part of the parties of a participation in the management of the company's affairs.

In *Re Elgindata Ltd* [1991] BCLC 959 the court held that a shareholder who acquires shares in a company cannot complain of unfairness if the management turns out to be poor. A shareholder cannot as part of his expectations insist on a reasonable standard of general management of a company. However, as it happened in *Re Elgindata Ltd* where the evidence showed that the managing director used assets of the company for his personal benefit and for the benefit of his family and friends and thereby reduced the whole of the petitioners shares, unfair prejudice was found and the court ordered the majority shareholder to buy out the minority.

Although Lord Hoffmann in the House of Lords decision of *O'Neill* v *Phillips* [1999] 1 WLR 1092, used the term 'legitimate expectation' from the area of public law he has now made it clear in *Re Saul D. Harrison* that the term 'legitimate expectation' should not be allowed to lead a life of its own and he intended the term to refer to traditional equitable principles. A court, according to his lordship, will not take into account the limited construction of the articles of association but would consider any other agreements that the parties may have arrived at and need to observe as a matter of good faith. The House of Lords also held in *O'Neill* that the section 459 remedy cannot be provided merely because the relationship between the parties has broken down and a minority shareholder should be able to exit. This is in line with the recommendations of the Law Commission Report on *Shareholder Remedies*.

Lord Hoffmann, also in *O'Neill*, stated that a balance has to be struck between the breadth of the discretion given to the court and the principle of legal certainty.

His Lordship acknowledged that if only the wider concept of fairness itself was used then petitions under section 459 that are often lengthy and expensive would become even more uncertain. In *O'Neill*, Lord Hoffmann also went onto state that 'legitimate expectation' cannot be taken to refer to an individual member's personal hope that other members will do something, which they have not in fact agreed to do.

In conclusion, it may be stated that the courts have become aware of the difficulties in allowing section 459 to be utilised without any clear guiding principles. The authorities here therefore set out the guiding principles in approaching what is to be considered as 'unfair prejudice'. The courts here also make it clear that they are mindful of not intervening too much in the company's commercial decision making. However, as recommended by the Law Commission in its Report *Shareholder Remedies*, there has to be better case management to deal with excessive length and costs. The Law Commission also recommended that in the most common type of case, exclusion from the management of a quasi-partnership, statutory presumptions should apply to simplify proceedings. The Law Commission recommended that if a petitioner held at least 10 per cent of the voting rights in the company and subsequently all the other members of the company were directors, and he was removed from management, a presumption of unfair prejudice will exist. The Law Commission was thus concerned with providing some degree of certainty for parties concerning the position a court is likely to take and enable cases to be dealt with more quickly when proceedings were commenced.

QUESTION 2

Through the words 'just and equitable' a court is enabled to recognise rights, expectations and obligations of members, *inter se*, and to wind up a company where such rights and obligations are being thwarted or obligations not observed even if what is being done is strictly within the law. Discuss.

Commentary

The question requires a discussion of the 'just and equitable' winding-up jurisdiction under section 122(1)(g) of the Insolvency Act 1986. What is essential here is to consider the approach of the courts to the just and equitable winding up before and after the leading case of *Ebrahimi* v *Westbourne Galleries Ltd* [1973] AC 360.

A good answer here would also consider critically the *Ebrahimi* decision itself and discuss whether it was correct to find a quasi-partnership.

Suggested Answer

The present section 122(1)(g) of the Insolvency Act 1986 permits a court to wind up a company where it is just and equitable to do so. The jurisdiction is one that is a legacy of partnership law. At one time the courts tended to identify special instances. For instance in *Loch* v *John Blackwood Ltd* [1924] AC 783, where the directors had failed to hold general meetings or submit accounts or recommend a dividend, the Privy Council held that the company could be wound up as there was a lack of confidence in the directors that had sprung from the lack of probity in the conduct of the company's affairs.

Another situation where a winding up would be ordered on the just and equitable ground is the loss of the company's substratum. In *Re German Date Coffee Co.* (1882) 20 ChD 169, the company's objects clause referred to the company exploiting a patent relating to a method of manufacturing date coffee. However, no patent was granted and the shareholders succeeded in winding up the company. The House of Lords in *Ebrahimi* v *Westbourne Galleries Ltd* [1973] AC 360, proceeded to deal with the use of the just and equitable winding-up jurisdiction in the context of the private company which is sometimes referred to by the label 'quasi-partnership'. The case concerned Mr Ebrahimi and Mr Nazar who had carried on business in partnership dealing in carpets. The business originally was run as a partnership till they had formed a private company carrying out the same business and the two of them were the original directors. Shortly after the incorporation Mr Nazar's son had become a director and between Mr Nazar and the son they held the majority of the shares and all the profits were distributed as directors' remuneration and no dividends were ever paid. Later Mr Ebrahimi was removed from the board by means of what is now section 303 of the Companies Act 1985.

Mr Ebrahimi succeeded in getting the court to wind up the company on the basis of it being just and equitable.

Lord Wilberforce identified certain circumstances in which equity would subject the exercise of legal rights to equitable considerations. The just and equitable jurisdiction, according to the House of Lords, ensures that one party cannot disregard the obligation he assumes in entering a particular type of company so as to insist on legal rights when it would be unjust or inequitable to insist upon those rights.

Lord Wilberforce identified the following characteristics of a company in which the court would recognise that legal rights are subject to equitable considerations:

(a)   A private company which is an association formed or continued on the basis of a personal relationship involving mutual confidence. It was suggested by Lord Wilberforce that such a relationship may be found when there was a pre-existing partnership.

(b)   An agreement or understanding that all or some shareholders shall participate in the conduct of the business.

(c)   Restrictions on the transfer of members' interests in the company. This would mean that if confidence is lost or if a member is removed from the board then he cannot take his stake and go elsewhere. Lord Wilberforce would acknowledge that the term quasi-partnership would be misleading. Since one is still concerned with a company it should be noted that it is from the law of partnerships that the conceptions of probity, good faith and mutual confidence were brought in when dealing with the just and equitable winding-up jurisdiction.

In *Ebrahimi* the House of Lords found that even though the legal power to remove a director by ordinary resolution was exercisable the majority were subject to obligations based on the expectations that all of them would be entitled to participate in management and this could be undermined.

The court found that on removal from the board not only did Mr Ebrahimi lose the right to participate in the company's management but also he could not earn his directors' remuneration. The case has always generated controversy as there was no indication at the time of the incorporation of the company that all the members were to have a right of participation in the management as there was no provision in the articles providing for weighted votes in the event of any attempts to remove a particular director from the board.

Further it could be argued that the three characteristics identified by Lord Wilberforce identifying a quasi-partnership could be found in almost all private companies. A company is different from a partnership in view of rights being defined in the Companies Act, the memorandum and the articles.

It would be possible to state today that based on the principle of the quasi-partnership in *Ebrahimi*, there is a single approach to dealing with the just and equitable winding up jurisdiction. What is required is evidence of a special underlying obligation to fellow members of good faith and confidence.

The later case of *Re A & B C Chewing Gum Ltd* [1975] 1 WLR 579, does establish that the underlying relationship can be found even if there is no pre-existing partnership. In the *A & B C Chewing Gum* case the petitioners were entitled by agreement with the company's directors to appoint a director to represent them on the board, and the directors subsequently refused to recognise an appointment by the petitioners. This entitled the court to wind up the company on the basis of it being just and equitable.

Although the decision has attracted criticism it may be a step in the right direction as in company law there is a need to identify the type of company which although it legally starts off with the structure of a company but is essentially run on the basis of trust and confidence and so is closer to a partnership. In *Clemens* v *Clemens Bros. Ltd* [1976] 2 All ER 268, Foster J relied on the *Ebrahimi* case to intervene to prevent a majority shareholder voting in a manner that was contrary to understandings with other members even though there was no statutory jurisdiction as there was no winding-up petition. It is also possible to state in the context of the quasi-partnership company that the relationship between members is a personal rather than a financial association.

QUESTION 3

In enacting sections 459 to 461 of the Companies Act 1985 there has been a virtual abolition of the rule in *Foss* v *Harbottle* which resulted in a great use of the remedy, which in turn has resulted in the courts adopting a restrictive approach to the concept of 'unfair prejudice'. Discuss.

Commentary

The question requires first of all a consideration of the law under section 210 of the Companies Act 1948 with its requirement to prove 'oppression' and the need also to show that as an alternative the company could be wound up on the ground of it being just and equitable.

The question also requires consideration of the rule in *Foss* v *Harbottle* and the difficulties plaintiffs face in bringing derivative actions to deal with maladministration. The answer should then focus on the elements of section 459, the remedies that the court can impose and how it has become more attractive to minority shareholders. It is as a result of this that the courts have taken a restrictive approach to the concept of 'unfair prejudice'. It would be necessary to analyse the decided cases in some detail to show the approach of the courts particularly in respect of commercial decision-making.

Suggested Answer

The remedy in sections 459 to 461 of the 1985 Companies Act replaced section 75 of the 1980 Companies Act which in turn replaced section 210 of the 1948

Companies Act. Section 210 of the 1948 Act was to implement the Cohen Committee's proposals.

The Cohen Committee had found that the court should be empowered to make such order as the court might think just instead of a winding-up order. The Department of Trade at that time misinterpreted the proposals and drafted section 210 in such a manner as to provide that an order under the section could only be made where the petitioner had made out a case for winding up on the 'just and equitable' ground. Section 210 was unsatisfactory as the petitioner had to establish that the affairs of the company were being conducted in a manner that was oppressive and this meant that a course of conduct had to be established that was 'harsh, burdensome and wrongful'.

It was very quickly realised that in cases where there has been misappropriation of the company's assets a petition under section 459 would be more successful than attempting to bring a derivative action based on the 'fraud on the minority' exception to the rule in *Foss* v *Harbottle*. In *Re London School of Electronics Ltd* [1986] Ch 211, the company ran courses in electronics. It was owned 25 per cent by the petitioner and 75 per cent by City Tutorial College Ltd which was in turn owned by two other individuals. The petitioner was a director of and a teacher in the London School of Electronics. There were differences between the petitioner and the other two individuals which resulted in the other two arranging for the students to be transferred to City Tutorial College Ltd. The court found that it was unfairly prejudicial to the interests of the petitioner as a member of the company for the students to be appropriated to City Tutorial College and the court ordered the shares of the petitioner to be bought by City Tutorial College, the majority shareholder.

The next decision which would also illustrate the width of the section 459 remedy today is *Re Elgindata Ltd* [1991] BCLC 959. In this case the petitioners made a wide variety of allegations such as exclusion from management, late payment of dividends, mismanagement and irresponsible expenditure by directors.

In his judgment, Warner J was prepared to hold that serious mismanagement can found conduct that is unfairly prejudicial to the interests of minority shareholders. Counsel in the course of his submissions referred to a passage in *Gore-Browne on Companies*, 44th ed. (1986) where the editors had referred to the intention of the Jenkins Committee to use the reformed statutory remedy which at that time was section 210 to be used to enforce directors' duty of care, although the courts had decided otherwise. Warner J, however, stated that generally a court would be reluctant to accept that managerial decisions can amount to unfairly prejudicial conduct. The reason for this is that a court is ill-qualified to deal with commercial decisions where there is disagreement between the majority who are in control of the company and the minority. The court also found that besides the issue of commercial judgment the other factors petitioners should realise is that they take the risk of the value of their shares being dependent on a measure of competence of the management.

It is therefore evident here that the courts have realised that there must be some limits on the extent to which a court can deal with matters of internal management. The other difficulty here is that petitioners often rely on the characteristics of a quasi-partnership set out by Lord Wilberforce in *Ebrahimi v Westbourne Galleries Ltd* [1973] AC 360. In *Re a Company (No. 005685 of 1988) (No. 2)* [1989] BCLC 427, Peter Gibson J stated that in most private companies the aspects of the quasi-partnership would be present but that does not necessarily show the existence of material confidence.

More recently in *Re Unisoft Group Ltd* (No. 3) [1994] 1 BCLC 609, Harman J noted that because of the range of section 459 every sort and kind of conduct over a period of a company's management will be gone over again in court. In the *Unisoft Group* case the court was not prepared to treat the breach of a shareholders' agreement in the passing of a resolution as conduct that was unfairly prejudicial to the interests of the member, if there was no prejudice in the commercial sense. The court was not prepared to accept any emotional prejudice, for instance, merely being removed from the board of directors.

In conclusion, it can be seen that the courts have become concerned with the extensive use of section 459 of the 1985 Companies Act. In the final analysis it could be said that so long as English company law relies on majority rule the increasing number of section 459 petitioners will be inevitable.

7 Maintenance of Capital

INTRODUCTION

A student coming to company law is often perplexed by the term 'capital'. There are two ways in which capital can be understood. One is 'share capital', which covers the share capital contributed by shareholders. The other is 'loan capital' which deals with what creditors contribute to enable the company to carry out its ordinary business.

In company law we speak of the 'rules' of maintenance of capital, and this would include matters such as a company not issuing shares at a discount, a company not being able to purchase its own shares and also reducing its capital only with the consent of the court.

In the area of capital reduction you should be aware of how, if there are preference shares which are entitled to priority in repayment of capital, then a return of capital to ordinary shareholders without having paid off the preference shares may be a variation of their rights. For further reading you should read ch. 10 of *Cases and Materials on Company Law* by Andrew Hicks and S.H. Goo. On the area of reform, students should now consider the consultation document of the DTI entitled *Modern Company Law for a Competitive Economy: the Strategic Framework* (London: DTI, 1999) paras 5.4.4 to 5.4.13.

QUESTION 1

'Every major Companies Act, beginning with the Act of 1867 has required that reduction of share capital ... should be confirmed by the court. [The House of Lords has repeatedly emphasised] that the courts had a discretion to confirm or not to confirm ... and that this discretion fell to be exercised by reference to the test of whether the scheme would be fair and equitable' (per Lord Cooper in *Scottish Insurance Corporation Ltd* v *Wilsons & Clyde Coal Co. Ltd* 1948 SC 360). Explain and comment.

Commentary

In dealing with the discussion of the passage, what has to be considered first is the question of what is 'fair and equitable' in terms of dealing with different classes of shareholders when there is capital reduction.

In this area you should aim to deal with how the different rights attaching to shares is a matter of construction as far as the terms of issue are concerned. Thus if the terms of issue are particularly silent, then a court would proceed on the basis of equality between shareholders. The answer should also deal with the workings of the present section 125 of the Companies Act when dealing with the variation of class rights.

Suggested Answer

In dealing with the passage by Lord Cooper it is important first to observe that a company may have different classes of members and their membership rights can under the articles be different. In the case of preference shareholders which we are concerned with in this question they are said to have 'preference shares' as the preference shareholder is entitled to an annual dividend per share which is paid in priority to any dividend payments to other members.

In respect of the winding-up position any agreement between a company and its members of a particular class concerning their class rights would be exhaustive since the preference share is more like a debenture with the company being entitled to return the capital at any time unless there are express provisions in the terms of the issue and the preference shareholders are not entitled to participate in the return of capital on the winding up. In the area of capital reduction the question would frequently arise as to whether the preference shareholders can remain so as to be able to participate in the distribution of surplus assets on a liquidation.

In the House of Lords decision of *Scottish Insurance Corporation Ltd* v *Wilsons & Clyde Coal Co. Ltd* [1949] AC 462, the company had to reduce its capital as its main asset, a colliery, was transferred to the National Coal Board as a result of nationalisation. The company was going to proceed to liquidation following the reduction of capital. The articles of association of the company provided that the preference shareholders would be entitled to a 7 per cent cumulative dividend and repayment of capital on winding up but there was no reference to distribution of surplus assets. The House of Lords held that the preference shareholders had no rights in the articles to paticipate in any surplus assets and it was possible for the company to reduce its capital by returning capital to preference shareholders.

The reduction of capital was therefore fair and equitable since the rights of preference and ordinary shareholders are set out in the articles and the articles were exhaustive of the rights of the preference shareholders in a winding up.

The approach here in the *Scottish Insurance Corporation* case is similar to the earlier Court of Appeal decision of *Re Chatterley-Whitfield Collieries Ltd* [1948] 2 All ER 593. The company here had also at the time of nationalisation to reduce capital in view of its colliery having been acquired. The Court of Appeal considered the rights of the preference shareholders in terms of the bargain between the company and preference shareholders, as only involving a right to receive a preferential dividend of an agreed amount and it was not unfair to oust them from the company. The Court of Appeal held in the *Chatterley-Whitfield* case that the preference shareholders had no rights to share in any surplus in the assets and that there was nothing inequitable in a reduction of capital to pay off preference shareholders first and it was also sound business practice since the preferential shareholders would be too burdensome in view of the reduction in the company's business.

The House of Lords decision of *Birch* v *Cropper* (1889) 14 App Cas 525 now has to be considered. Here a company had been wound up, leaving a surplus of assets after paying all debts and returning capital to members. It was held that since the articles of association were silent on the distribution of the surplus assets, there was a presumption of equality between different classes of shareholders. To the House of Lords the principle that is applicable is that every person who becomes a member of a company limited by shares of equal amount becomes entitled to a proportionate part in the capital of the company, including uncalled capital, unless it be otherwise provided by the regulation of the company. Turning now to the question of variation of class rights, section 135 of the Companies Act 1985 provides for the procedure on the alteration of class rights. In the case of capital reduction, if the class rights are stated in a company's memorandum without any provision in the memorandum or articles for variation then the class rights can be varied only with the unanimous consent of the members, under section 125(5).

On the issue of variation of class rights, by section 125(8), 'variation' is also meant to cover abrogation of the rights.

As discussed above, whenever there is a reduction of capital and return of capital takes place, these would only be a variation of class rights if the cancellation of preference shares abrogates the rights of preference shareholders to participate in the surplus of the company's assets. If on the other hand there is no right to participate in the surplus of the company's assets then there would be no abrogation of the preference shareholders' rights.

In *House of Fraser plc v ACGE Investments Ltd* [1987] AC 387, the House of Lords held that if capital is reduced by returning all capital to a class of preference shareholders, thus expelling them from the company, this would not be a variation of the preference shareholders' rights. For class rights to be varied it is the nature of the rights that should be affected not their enjoyment.

In conclusion, it can be stated that the courts have taken a very narrow and technical view of the rights of preference shareholders in the area of class rights. In *Re Northern Engineering Industries plc* [1994] BCC 618, the articles of association of the company specifically referred to rights being varied when there is a reduction in the capital paid up on preference shares. This then meant that a class meeting had to be held.

QUESTION 2

The share capital of Animals Ltd (the company) consists of £500,000 divided into 400,000 £1 ordinary shares and 100,000 £1 6 per cent preference shares. The preference shares have a right to participate £1 per share out of any surplus on a winding up. The preference shares are also fully participating as to dividends. The directors of Animals Ltd now find that the importation and sale of animals as pets is not doing that well, and want to negotiate terms for the repayment of capital to the preference shareholders and eliminate them from the company. The negotiations have not been succcessful as a majority of the preference shareholders do not accept the proposal. The directors now seek your advice on the following two proposals, namely:

Proposal 1

To issue a further 300,000 shares with rights identical to those of the existing preference shares to persons who support the directors of the company so that they would vote in favour of the directors' proposals at a class meeting of the preference shareholders who would in turn vote to eliminate the class of shareholders.

Proposal 2

The directors want to cause a special resolution to be passed reducing the company's capital by 20 per cent in accordance with a scheme in terms of which the preference shareholders are to be repaid the full nominal value of their shares and are to be eliminated as shareholders.

Advise the directors.

Commentary

Here you have to be able to deal with each of the proposals of the directors and you would have to compare the relative merits of the proposals. The question does not merely deal with class rights and the area of capital reduction, but also the manner in which shareholders vote at the general meeting on alteration of the articles and class meetings.

In dealing with the merits of the first proposal it is also necessary to consider the exercise of directors' powers on the issue of shares. The question is yet another example of how in the subject of company law it is difficult often to pigeon-hole topics.

Suggested Answer

In dealing with the advice to the directors of the company, it would be necessary to consider each of the proposals in turn.

Proposal 1

The general principle in company law is that whenever a shareholder votes at a general meeting, he can vote in his own self-interest. This was held to be the position in *North-West Transportation Co. Ltd* v *Beatty* (1887) 12 App Cas 589. The Privy Council held that a decision by the shareholders is a decision that is binding on the company and a shareholder is perfectly entitled to vote upon any question in his self-interest. However, the meeting that is to be held here is a class meeting. This is the case as the preference shareholders have separate rights as to the dividends and the right to participate in the surplus on a winding up. In a class meeting it has been held that a member who is voting must vote in what is in the interest of the class of members. In *Re Holders Investment Trust Ltd* [1971] 1 WLR 583, it was held that the power of the majority to bind the minority must be exercised for the purpose of benefiting the class as a whole, not only particular members.

The clear intention of proposal 1 is that the new preference shareholders are not to vote in the interests of their class. There is another difficulty here and that is if the directors do proceed to issue the further preference shares purely for the purposes of gaining control at the class meeting the exercise of the power to issue shares could be challenged.

In *Hogg* v *Cramphorn Ltd* [1967] Ch 254, it was held that directors' powers to issue shares, although exercised bona fide, must not be exercised for improper purposes. The same was held by the Privy Council in *Howard Smith Ltd* v *Ampol Petroleum Ltd* [1974] AC 821, where the Privy Council rejected the view that a power exercised by directors would be valid so long as it has been exercised bona fide in the interest of the company, which could be said to be the case in this problem in view of the downturn of the business and the need to eliminate the preference shareholders.

Thus since the *Howard Smith* case and *Hogg* v *Cramphorn Ltd*, the courts proceed on the basis that the purpose of the power to issue shares is to raise capital and any exercise of the power which is not for that purpose would be invalid. The directors should therefore be advised here that leaving aside the issue of voting at class meetings, the preference shareholders can also challenge the validity of the issue of the further 300,000 shares.

Proposal 2

By section 135(2)(c) of the Companies Act 1985 the company here can pass a special resolution for reducing the share capital by paying off the paid up share capital which is in excess of its wants. However even if the company is in a position to secure the special majority there is the need to obtain the consent of the court under section 136 of the Companies Act 1985. Although the procedure of obtaining the consent of the court may appear to the directors as a matter of ensuring that creditors' interests are protected and there are no real objections from creditors, there is also a need to ensure that no class rights are being varied within the meaning of section 125 of the Companies Act 1985. Section 125(3)(c) of the Act requires that if there is any capital reduction that is connected with the variation of class rights then the procedure in section 125(2)(a) or (b) must be followed together with any requirements of the memorandum or articles in relation to the variation. What has to be considered next is whether the paying off of the preference shareholders can be treated as a variation of class rights.

Section 125(8) provides for the provisions on the variation of rights to apply where there is also the abrogation of their rights. The preference shareholders could argue here that if there is to be any return of capital in view of the decrease in the company's business then it should be the ordinary shareholders whose capital should be returned first as the preference shareholders have a right to remain as shareholders till the stage at which the company is wound up as they have a right to priority on any surplus on a winding up.

The present facts can be distinguished from the House of Lords decision of *Scottish Insurance Corporation Ltd* v *Wilsons & Clyde Coal Co. Ltd* [1949] AC 462. In the *Scottish Insurance* case the articles did not give preference shareholders any rights in relation to return of any surplus assets on winding up of the company. Here preference shareholders have a right to have priority with regard to any surplus assets on winding up. In *Scottish Insurance* the House of Lords emphasised that before confirming a capital reduction the court would ensure that it is going to be equitable. In view of section 125 which deals with the position of class rights, the company here would have to comply with section 125(2)(a) or (b), that is, there must be at least a class meeting with the preference shareholders passing an extraordinary resolution or three-quarters of the holders of the nominal value of the preference shares consenting in writing.

In conclusion the directors should be advised that there is no possibility of carrying out either of the two proposals.

QUESTION 3

A limited company not in liquidation can make no payment by way of return of capital to its shareholders except as a step in an authorised reduction of capital. Any other payment made by it by means of which it parts with moneys to its shareholders must and can only be made by way of dividing profits. Explain and comment.

Commentary

The question requires you to consider the principle of maintenance of capital. A useful starting-point is the statutory duty now imposed by section 74 of the Insolvency Act 1986 on a shareholder contributing towards the assets of the company to the extent of the nominal value of the shares and then dealing with the checks the law has introduced to ensure that there is no unlawful return of capital. It is also necessary to comment on whether the provisions in the law dealing with the maintenance of capital are satisfactory.

Suggested Answer

Under section 74 of the Insolvency Act 1986 a member of a company has a statutory liability to contribute to the assets of a company when it is wound up. In the Court of Appeal decision of *Guinness v Land Corporation of Ireland* (1882) 22 ChD 349, Cotton LJ, when commenting upon what is now section 74 of the Insolvency Act 1986, stated that the capital of the company is a fund to pay the creditors in the event of winding up. Also Cotton LJ went on to state that whatever has been paid as the capital by the members cannot be returned to them, and that the capital identified in the memorandum can only be employed for the objects of the company. It would now be necessary to consider the ways in which the legislature has ensured that there is no side-stepping of the principles as to maintenance of capital. As early as the case of *Trevor v Whitworth* (1887) 12 App Cas 409, the House of Lords had held that a reduction of capital other than permitted by statute is illegal. Today no reduction of capital can be made except in the mode and to the extent for which express provision is made by the Companies Act 1985. Section 135 of the Companies Act 1985 permits a company to carry out a reduction of capital if its articles permit it do so and it is confirmed by the court.

The modern legislation has come to extend the provisions on capital reduction to the share premium account and the capital redemption reserve. To protect the position of creditors there is a statutory procedure by which the interests of creditors are protected if there is a diminution of members' liability to pay uncalled capital or a repayment of capital to members. These provisions are contained in section 136(2) to (6) and section 137(1).

It was held in *Re Meux's Brewery Co. Ltd* [1919] 1 Ch 28, that creditors can only object if there is a strong reason to do so, namely, if the company is reducing its capital in a manner whereby it is parting with its means of paying its creditors. The procedure in relation to creditors is that a list must be prepared of creditors as at a date fixed by the court. By section 136 the creditors on the list would be creditors whose debts can be proved in a winding up on the day fixed by the court. The court would only confirm the reduction if each creditor positively consents or the company has made provision for paying the creditor.

Since the Companies Act 1980, if a reduction of a public company's capital has the effect of bringing the nominal value of its allotted share capital below £50,000 then the company must be re-registered as a private company and by section 139(1) and (2) and section 118(1) of the Companies Act 1985 the registrar of companies must not register the reduction of capital unless the change of status takes place. It is also possible for the order of court confirming the capital reduction to direct the change of status.

The other development since the 1980 Companies Act, and which is now found in section 142 of the 1985 Companies Act is the obligation on the part of directors of a public company to call an extraordinary general meeting within 28 days of a director first becoming aware of the fact that the net assets have fallen to half or less of the called-up share capital. The object of the meeting is to consider what measures should be taken to deal with that situation. It is a criminal offence if a director knowingly and wilfully fails to comply with these requirements.

The next area that has to be considered in the context of the rule relating to the preservation of capital is in respect of the payment of dividends. The basic problem here is that a company normally does not keep its funds in cash, and its assets in non-cash form are continually changing so that the value of these assets fluctuate. The assets may be increased by profits or diminished by losses.

For a long time the courts were working with general principles such as a dividend not to be paid out of capital. Also the courts tried to keep the issue of how profits were calculated as a matter of business practice and did not want to interevene. However, since the 1980 Companies Act and by sections 263 to 281 of the Companies Act 1985 there are statutory rules restricting what the Act terms as distributions, which would cover 'every description of distribution of a company's assets to its members whether in cash or otherwise'.

In the case of *Aveling Barford Ltd* v *Perion Ltd* (1989) 5 BCC 677, a sale at an undervalue of an asset of Aveling Barford Ltd to another company controlled by the sole beneficial shareholder of Aveling Barford was held to be a distribution to him. In essence what the statutory rules now ensure is that any distribution by a company must be out of its accumulated realised profits that have not been utilised by distribution or capitalisation, less its accumulated, realised losses so far as not previously written off in a reduction or reorganisation of capital duly made. This is provided for by section 263(3). It is now no longer possible, as was done at one time, to distribute profits of one year despite not making up losses in previous years. As for the consequences of excessive distribution, the directors who authorised the payment are liable to repay the money to the company. This is the common law position and was held to be the case in *Re Exchange Banking Co., Flitcroft's Case* (1882) 21 ChD 519.

Under section 277(1) of the 1985 Companies Act every member is liable to repay a distribution he has received if he knew, or had reasonable grounds for knowing, that it was being paid in contravention of the Companies Act's provisions. It is also useful to note that in the case of *Aveling Barford*, Hoffmann J went on to state that the transaction at undervalue was a sham and an unlawful return of capital and no ratification by shareholders could validate the transaction unless approved by the court. There would be in the circumstances some authority for the proposition that if there is a transaction with a shareholder at an undervalue, even if entered into by the directors honestly and even if the transaction is within the company's powers, it can be later challenged by a liquidator or an administrative receiver.

In conclusion, it may be said that despite the great lengths to which the legislature has gone to ensure the maintenance of capital, in reality in many private companies it is directors' remuneration that has to be watched. The complex accounting rules to ensure that distributions are within the law would be of little assistance. The other difficulty is that since there are no minimum capital requirements in relation to private companies businesses are often under-capitalised and the availability of the company's capital as a guarantee fund is not very helpful.

QUESTION 4

Kelong Ltd is a company formed by various football fans who want to develop computer games relating to the organising of world cup matches, and the progress of the teams that can be controlled by the players. The authorised capital of the company is 150,000 shares divided into 95,000 £1 ordinary shares, 50,000 preference shares and 5,000 £1 deferred shares.

The memorandum of association also goes on to provide:

(a)   The preference shares shall carry rights to a 14 per cent cumulative preference dividend while the company is a going concern and priority to a return of capital on a winding up.

(b)   The preference shares shall carry rights to vote on the issue of whether the company shall go into voluntary liquidation but, save as aforesaid, shall carry no rights to vote in general meetings.

(c)   The deferred shares rank *pari passu* with the ordinary shares as regards dividends but only after the ordinary shares have received an annual 12 per cent dividend and as regards return of capital in a winding up the deferred shares shall be subordinated to all other classes of capital.

The articles of association are in the form of Table A. All the authorised capital has been issued and is spread out among 10 different people, the largest single shareholder is Vanna, who holds 30,000 ordinary shares and 20,000 preference shares. The business has now begun to fail and the directors realise that capital has been lost and they want first of all to cancel the deferred shares which are unrepresented by available assets. They have also been advised that the preference dividend has to be reduced from 14 per cent to 8 per cent.

The directors have found that most of the ordinary shareholders, in the region of 85 per cent , and also the same percentage of preference shareholders support the proposals. It is the 15 per cent of both classes that are likely to oppose the cancellation. Also all the deferred shareholders oppose the cancellation. Advise the directors.

Commentary

This is one of those questions where the length often puts off students. The advice here is to go through the question line by line to identify the relevant issues.

In reading this question it will become apparent that it concerns capital reduction. The directors would want advice on the procedure and also on the position of holding class meetings. The question of class meetings would also raise the issue of whether any class rights are affected. It is also necessary to consider in which priority capital can be repaid to shareholders.

Suggested Answer

It will be necessary first to consider the attempt of the directors to bring about a reduction of capital.

Reduction of Capital by Cancellation of the Deferred Shares

In dealing with capital reduction the Court of Appeal in *Re Chatterley-Whitfield Collieries Ltd* [1948] 2 All ER 593 proceeded on the basis of looking for a business answer to the question, such as the facts here. If capital has been lost and if the company is looking at an alternative to winding up then the deferred shares would be the first to go. Deferred shares are vulnerable to cancellation first as these shares are entitled to substantial returns after the ordinary shareholders have received the dividends.

The company could by special resolution reduce its capital under section 135. The company would have to seek the confirmation of the resolution by the court, and since the resolution would involve the payment to shareholders of paid-up share capital, the procedure for consulting creditors would have to be followed unless the court dispensed with it. The deferred shareholders have no rights to remain as shareholders. There is no question of unfairness here as, just like preference shareholders who have no rights to participate in any surplus of assets, the deferred shareholders are to be dealt with on the same basis as in a winding up. Thus according to the memorandum of association here the ordinary shareholders and other classes have got priority in a winding up. Essentially it would be, as stated in the Court of Appeal decision of *Re Chatterley-Whitfield Colleries Ltd*, financial ineptitude if the company did not take steps to reduce its capital by paying off the deferred shareholders who would not be able to earn their keep.

Alteration of Class Rights

The decision to reduce the preference dividend from 14 per cent to 8 per cent would not be a reduction of capital. This is the case as there is no cancellation of any capital, or return of capital to shareholders.

However, the move to reduce the percentage of dividend is an alteration of class rights. Class rights can be defined as the rights which attach to a particular class of shares. The rights that attach to the preference shares are in the memorandum and cover also priority to a return of capital on winding up.

Since the 1980 Companies Act there are statutory provisions to deal with the variation of class rights. On our facts here the rights are contained in the memorandum and by virtue of section 125(5) of the Companies Act 1985 if rights are contained in the memorandum and if the memorandum and articles do not contain provisions with respect to the variation of those rights, then those rights may be varied if all the members of the company agree to the variation.

It would also be necessary here to consider the holding of class meetings and the way in which voting is to take place. At class meetings the power of the majority to bind the minority must be exercised for the purpose of benefiting the class as a whole. In *Re Holders Investment Trust Ltd* [1971] 1 WLR 583, the Court of Appeal held that the question of what is for the benefit of the class as a whole has to be considered.

This would mean that when we take the position of Vanna here, the majority shareholder, he may vote in terms of considering what may be in the interests of the company as a whole. This would put him in a position of conflict of interest. The resolution passed in such circumstances would be invalid. On the facts it would be difficult for Vanna to show that he had voted bona fide in the belief that he was acting in the interests of the general body of the class of members.

Court-sanctioned Arrangement

It would also be possible for the directors to obtain a court order to have a scheme proposed to the deferred shareholders. This can be treated as coming within the meaning of 'compromise' in section 425 of the Act. The court can consider a scheme so long as it is not *ultra vires* and the company must also provide a quid pro quo for the abandonment of rights or claims.

In *Re NFU Development Trust Ltd* [1972] 1 WLR 1548, the court held that a proposal that nearly all members of the company should surrender their membership without compensation was not a compromise and not an arrangement within the meaning of section 425 of the Companies Act 1985.

On the facts here it is evident that the company is not going to be in any financial position to offer compensation to the deferred shareholders. Furthermore the court could not sanction the scheme unless it was agreed to at a class meeting by a majority of the deferred shareholders representing three-fourths in value of the class, which would be impossible as all members of the class oppose the scheme.

8 Companies Purchasing Their Own Shares

INTRODUCTION

This is an area of the law which is part of the company's duty to preserve its capital. In the case of *Trevor* v *Whitworth* (1887) 12 App Cas 409, it was held that a company may not purchase its own shares because that would amount to returning the capital contributed for the purchased shares.

Section 143(1) of the Companies Act 1985 contains the principle in *Trevor* v *Whitworth* (1887). You should also be aware of sections 151 to 155 of the Companies Act. Further it is also necessary to appreciate the current version of the provisions to be aware of the moves taken to reduce the strictness of the provisions particularly from the time of the late 1970s to encourage investment in small companies by allowing members wishing to recover their investment in shares to be paid out by the company.

There is a useful section in ch. 10 of *Cases and Materials on Company Law*, A. Hicks and S.H. Goo.

QUESTION 1

Assess the present law on financial assistance contained in sections 151 to 158 of the Companies Act 1985. Is there any rational policy running through the legislation or case law?

Commentary

The question requires a consideration of the provisions relating to the prohibition on a company giving financial assistance directly or indirectly in the acquisition of its own shares. It would be important here to deal with the House of Lords decision in *Brady* v *Brady* [1989] AC 755. Also the loophole in the section disclosed by the decision of *Arab Bank plc* v *Merchantile Holdings Ltd* [1994] Ch 71.

Suggested Answer

It is generally illegal for a company to give financial assistance either directly or indirectly for the acquisition of its own shares or the shares in its holding company. Although this is the general rule the Companies Act 1985 recognises certain exceptions such as financing employee share schemes, redeeming or repurchasing shares under a scheme approved by the members, and paying up an issue of bonus shares.

However, our concern here is more in terms of the prohibition and the circumstances where the assistance can be given legitimately under the Companies Act. If one considers why the law prohibits such financial assistance to start with it would be found that, although such assistance may not be a reduction of the issued share capital, it does threaten the assets of the company.

The most common type of situation where the question of financial assistance exists is where there is to be a takeover. Financial assistance would arise here if the takeover is to be financed out of the company's own assets once control is obtained.

Section 152 of the Act provides a detailed definition of 'financial assistance' and it has also been further stated in *Charterhouse Investment Trust Ltd* v *Tempest Diesels Ltd* [1986] BCLC 1 that although the term 'giving financial assistance' has no technical meaning it must be given a meaning in accordance with commercial relations and also at the same time a court has to be careful as the section is a penal one.

It must be borne in mind that whilst it is stated above that the meaning of financial assistance must be construed from the standpoint of commercial realities, from the point of view of business people and their advisers sections 151 to 158 can at times bring about technical distinctions that are not so comprehensible. For instance, if one is purchasing shares and as security one's land is mortgaged to pay the price, this is acceptable under the law. Also the shares themselves can be used as collateral for a mortgage. However, if a takeover bidder, having acquired all the shares in a company, mortgages the company's sole asset which is the piece of land, that would be unlawful financial assistance. This is the case as the piece of land has been used as security for the bank loan that provided the funds to buy the shares.

The distinction between the two situations above can be technical and perplexing to the lay person and does require the consideration of whether there is any sound policy consideration in the various provisions prohibiting financial assistance. Looking at the current provisions it may be said that, by section 153, what is not prohibited is financial assistance given in good faith in the interests of the company if the 'principal purpose' is not the acquisition of the shares or such acquisition is an 'incidental part of some larger purpose of the company'.

It is this exception that has to be considered carefully as in practical terms it is not very certain how it is to be interpreted.

In *Brady* v *Brady* [1989] AC 755, the House of Lords had to consider this meaning of 'incidental part of some larger purpose of the company' exception. The case concerned a family business of road haulage and the manufacture and distribution of drinks through a private company, T. Brady & Sons Ltd. The company was run by two brothers who could not after a while work with one another.

It was decided by those advising the two brothers that it would be better if the business as a going concern was split up into two businesses with one of the brothers 'J' taking up the haulage side of the business and the other brother 'B' the drinks side of the business. It was also part of a complex scheme that a payment be made to balance the difference in values.

A company, M Ltd, controlled by 'J', was also incorporated to receive assets from Brady Ltd to help pay for the shares acquired by it in Brady.

The issue of financial assistance arose when 'B' refused to go ahead with the agreement and 'J' sued for specific performance. 'B' resisted on the ground that the transaction was unlawful financial assistance. 'J' had argued that the transaction was exempted within section 153(2)(a) as the larger purpose was the resolving of the deadlock between the brothers. The Court of Appeal was divided on the interpretation of what was the company's principal purpose. The difficulty which the House of Lords also experienced here was that although it was readily accepted that the assistance that M Ltd received from Brady was financial assistance within section 151(2) the question now was whether the company could rely on section 153(2). On the question of whether the assistance was 'in good faith in the interests of the company' the court concluded that that must be tested according to the genuine belief of those providing assistance and could be satisfied here as if the scheme was not implemented. Brady's business could ultimately be broken up if the deadlock persisted and Brady Ltd had to be wound up. However, on the requirement of a larger purpose the House of Lords was not prepared to consider the view of those deciding the interests of the company and an objective test was preferred. The House of Lords looked at the mischief which the law wanted to deal with and that was to prevent assistance that had as its object reducing the indebtedness of a purchaser of shares. Section 153 was traced to the case of *Belmont Finance Corporation* v *Williams Furniture Ltd (No. 2)* [1980] 1 All ER 393. This meant, according to the House of Lords, the object was to permit genuine commercial transactions, such as when the purchaser of shares in a company purchases an asset from another company in the ordinary course of business and through that purchase of an asset is able to reduce its indebtedness.

In the *Brady* decision the House of Lords considered that the reasons for the assistance could not be treated as a commercial purpose. One could question here why this could not be the case as it was the only way Brady Ltd could carry on in business while the business was split into two and also that if there was any assistance it was incidental.

The difficulty with the *Brady* decision is that it made illegal a transaction which from the point of view of the declared aims of the law is not supposed to be illegal. It is difficult to see a consistent policy here. Also parties wanting to avoid section 151 intentionally can put together a genuine commercial transaction to achieve the result of providing financial assistance. The litigation in *Brady* was later shown to be unnecessary as Brady being a private company could provide assistance so long as it was solvent which it was and complied with the requirements in section 155. The important point to note here is that Brady's advisers were clearly aware of this possibility but had proceeded on the basis that any assistance here was only incidental to a larger purpose. One is reminded of the comments of Peter Holland, a practising solicitor, when he wrote in the *Gazette* in 1993 (vol. 90, No. 45, p. 23) that section 151 is 'most quoted by practising company lawyers as wasting more time and causing more anguish than any other company law requirement'.

It could be said in conclusion that in view of the various exemptions created over the years there is very little to be gained by retaining such a rule as section 151 of the Companies Act 1985. More recently another loophole in the legislation has been exposed. In *Arab Bank plc* v *Merchantile Holdings Ltd* [1994] Ch 71 it was held that section 151 has no extraterritorial effects. Further whilst section 153 is supposed to exempt genuine commercial transactions in the interests of the company the litigation in *Brady* has not certainly shown that to be the case.

QUESTION 2

A plc is a company specialising in the manufacture of electronic toys. It has two wholly owned subsidiaries, B Ltd and C Ltd, which actually operate quite independently of A plc. A plc, however, does depend on the supply of circuit boards from B Ltd and C Ltd for its toy factory.

It has now been discovered by the directors of B Ltd that it is time for the company to improve the production methods at its plant and a new computer system is required to run the machinery. It has also come to light that Leeson a 15 per cent holder of the shares in A plc can sell the computer system at a special price of £120,000 to B Ltd. Also C Ltd can lend £20,000 to B Ltd in respect of this. The directors of B Ltd now decide at a board meeting that they will purchase the computer system from Leeson because the price is especially low, and also it is known that Leeson would use the proceeds of the sale to increase his holding of A plc by 3 per cent. The increase by Leeson of his shareholding is something that the directors of B Ltd want to encourage as they believe that this would discourage a takeover bid by a foreign manufacturer, Dawoo Ltd of Japan. Advise the board of directors of B Ltd.

Commentary

The question deals with the interpretation of section 151 of the Companies Act 1985 and the impact of the House of Lords decision of *Brady* v *Brady*.

Suggested Answer

The directors of B Ltd would have to consider the possibility of there being an infringement of section 151. Here Leeson is interested in acquiring further shares in A plc and B Ltd's purchase of the computer system can be assistance indirectly for the purpose of that acquisition. Section 151(1) provides that it would not be lawful for a company to provide assistance directly or indirectly for the purpose of acquiring shares in the company or its holding company. The directors here would be concerned with any breach of section 151 as the contravention is a criminal offence. The directors here have to be advised that section 151 does not prohibit a company from giving the assistance if, by section 153(2), the acquisition of shares is an 'incidental part' of some larger purpose of the company and, by section 153(2)(b), the assistance is given in good faith in the interests of the company.

It would be necessary first of all to consider what is meant by in the 'interests of the company'.

In the leading case of *Brady* v *Brady*, at the Court of Appeal stage ([1988] BCLC 20), it was accepted that the 'interests of the company' would cover the company's commercial interests and interests of the employees.

On our facts it could be stated that preventing the takeover by a foreign manufacturer could be said to be in the long-term interests of A plc as a commercial concern. In turn this would also be in the interests of B Ltd as B Ltd is a wholly owned subsidiary and a takeover of A plc would allow any competitor to damage the group of companies.

The next point that has to be considered is whether the purpose here is financial assistance in itself or whether the financial assistance is an incidental purpose of some larger purpose. Here again the *Brady* decision has to be considered. In the House of Lords [1989] AC 755, Lord Oliver of Aylmerton had held that the section was difficult to construe. To Lord Oliver section 153(2)(a) contemplated two alternative solutions. The first envisaged a principal and a subsidiary purpose. The second aspect is whether financial assistance was intended to achieve any object other than the reduction or discharge of the indebtedness but that result is merely incidental to some larger purpose.

Here it could be said that the purpose is to enable B Ltd to improve its computer system so that it can improve its means of production and this could be treated as the larger purpose with any financial assistance being only incidental. It is also useful to note here that the present provision in section 153(2) was initially introduced after the Court of Appeal decision in *Belmont Finance Corporation v Williams Furniture (No. 2)* [1980] 1 All ER 393, so as to ensure that genuine commercial transactions would not be caught by the Act.

In the *Belmont Finance Corporation* case the suspected transaction concerned the purchase of a company by Belmont at an inflated price, the consideration for the transaction being the share capital in Belmont itself. It was emphasised by the Court of Appeal in the case that, even if valid commercial reasons existed at the time for the deal, if any part of its purpose was to provide financial assistance then it would be caught by the then section preventing financial assistance which was section 54 of the Companies Act 1948. The Court of Appeal in *Belmont* had found clear evidence that the transaction was an exceptional and artificial transaction. However, what was envisaged by Buckley LJ in the course of his judgment in the *Belmont Finance* case was that the acquisition from the purchaser of the shares of some asset which the company requires for its ordinary business should not be treated as illegal.

In order therefore to make the position clear section 42 of the Companies Act 1981 introduced what is now section 153(2)(a) and (b) of the Companies Act 1985.

The directors of B Ltd could therefore be confidently advised that the larger purpose is to acquire at a good price the computer system, so as to improve the production facilities of the company. The providing of any assistance, it could be said here, is like a by-product of the larger purpose rather than an independent purpose.

The directors here can further be advised that if the prescribed statutory procedure in sections 156, 157 and 158 is followed then by the passing of a special resolution assistance can come outside section 151.

9 Loan Capital

INTRODUCTION

In this chapter we are concerned with probably the most common way companies raise capital for business activities and that is through borrowing. The lender would want security for the loan and this is provided by way of a debenture. Debentures are documents that evidence a debt and the company creates charges that are either fixed or floating charges.

The definition of the floating charge and particularly how it can be compared with a fixed charge is particularly important for an understanding of this area of the law. You should also be aware of priorities when the company is being wound up and the effect of the Insolvency Act 1986 on the setting aside of charges, transactions at undervalue and preferences.

QUESTION 1

Define what is meant by a 'floating charge' and how it can be distinguished from a 'fixed charge'.

Commentary

The question requires the characteristics of a floating charge to be considered and to distinguish the 'fixed charge'. The answer should concentrate on how the law only provides general guidelines.

Suggested Answer

The floating charge first can be identified as a charge over the company's assets which would 'float' till there is some intervention by the creditor, when the charge crystallises. In *Re Yorkshire Woolcombers Association Ltd* [1903] 2 Ch 284, Romer LJ said that floating charge is not a legal term but rather one that has to be interpreted in the context of the then Companies Act 1900 by considering three characteristics namely:

(a)   if the charge is on a class of assets of a company present and future;

(b)   if that class is one which in the ordinary course of the business of the company would be changing from time to time; and

(c)   if you find that by the charge it is contemplated that until some future step is taken by or on behalf of those interested in the charge, the company may carry on its business in the ordinary way as far as concerns the particular class of assets.

By contrast a specific charge is a charge on a specific item of property. In *Illingworth v Houldsworth* [1904] AC 355, Lord Macnaghten stated that a specific charge is one that fastens on ascertained and definite property or property capable of being ascertained and defined.

In *Evans v Rival Granite Quarries Ltd* [1910] 2 KB 979, a judgment had been given against the quarry company for a debt. The company was owed money by the bank and a judgment creditor obtained a garnishee order against the bank. Evans had a charge on the quarry to secure a debt which was due and payable but Evans had not taken any steps to crystallise his charge. When he heard of the garnishee order he told the bank that as chargee of the company's property he was entitled to the money and it could not be attached by garnishee proceedings. It was held that Evans was not entitled to the money as he had no specific charge on any assets of the company. The court held here that if Evans wanted the money he should have appointed a receiver in order to crystallise his floating charge. The court held that a floating charge is a floating mortgage applying to every item comprised in the security, but not specifically affecting any until some crystallising event occurs. The floating chargee does have a present interest in the subject-matter of the charge before it crystallises and so can, for example, obtain an injunction to prevent the company dealing with its assets otherwise than in the normal course of its business.

In dealing with particular types of assets it has been difficult for creditors to establish a fixed charge on the company's book debts. The reason is that although the document creating a charge on book debts would be described as a 'fixed charge', it would be treated as a floating charge if it contemplates that the company will be free to use in its business the money it collects from its debtors, without reference to the chargee.

To create a fixed charge on book debts it is necessary for the money collected from the company's debtors to be held for the chargee. In *William Gaskell Group Ltd* v *Highley* [1994] 1 BCLC 197, a charge on book debts which required them to be paid into a special account from which withdrawals could not be made without the chargee's consent was treated as a fixed charge.

In *Re CCG International Enterprises Ltd* [1993] BCLC 1428, a contract giving to a bank a floating charge on a company's assets required the company to insure all the charged assets and required any money received under the insurance policy to be paid into an account designated by the bank and used as the bank directed either to reduce the debt secured by the charge or to replace the lost assets. It was held that this created a fixed charge on the insurance money.

The floating charge, it can be seen, was invented in order to provide a means of charging a company's current assets. The advantage of the floating charge is that the company can use its current assets in such a way as to convert them into cash and so as to acquire new assets. The floating charge also thus allows the company to sell its assets freely, and persons can deal with the company with certainty.

In conclusion it could be stated that the floating charge can be analysed as a charge coupled with a licence to the company to deal with each asset without reference to the chargee though only in the normal course of the company's business.

QUESTION 2

Ramos Ltd is a company specialising in import and export of goods. The company, however, ran into financial difficulties and it went into a creditors' voluntary liquidation. The assets that have been realised are about £40,000. The company owes over £200,000 to Flora, a Filipino company, secured by a debenture. The debenture contains the following:

(a)   a 'first specific equitable charge' over freehold and leasehold property;

(b)   a first specific charge on all book debts and other debts now or at any time during the continuance of this security due or owing to the company.

Flora had served notice on the company to crystallise its charge over the book debts. The liquidator now seeks your advice on the following matters, first whether the book debts should be applied to pay the Commissioners of Customs and Excise in priority to Flora, and secondly if the charge over the book debts can be treated as a fixed charge.

Commentary

The question is a 'problem' type question testing your understanding of the distribution between 'fixed' and 'floating' charges. What has to be also covered is the position with regard to preferential debts.

Suggested Answer

It would be necessary first to consider the issue of the nature of the charge, to decide whether there is a fixed or floating charge over book debts. In the Court of Appeal decision of *Re Yorkshire Woolcombers Association Ltd* [1903] 2 Ch 284, the court identified three characteristics which a floating charge has to possess. They are first the nature of the goods which must cover present and future assets, secondly the charge should also be dormant until the undertaking charged ceases to be a going concern or until the person in whose favour the charge is created intervenes, and thirdly the asset must be of a class that the company would be charging in its ordinary course of business.

In this case although the document creating the charge refers to the charge being a 'specific charge' the test is one of considering the substance and not the form. The court in *Re Brightlife Ltd* [1987] Ch 200 held that a charge had to be characterised according to the law. The debts here are ones that the company is free to deal with when the debts are realised.

In *Re New Bullas Trading Ltd* [1994] 1 BCLC 485, the lenders had provided in the debenture that money received by a company in respect of a book debt was to be paid into a specified bank account where it had to be dealt with by the company in accordance with written directions. The court found that the intention of the parties was to create an equitable charge over the present book debts and held that such a charge can be an equitable assignment.

The next issue to be considered is whether the charge can be treated as crystallised by the serving of the notice. The controversy here is whether crystallisation only takes place on the appointment of a receiver or in the event when the company stops trading or whether parties can agree crystallisation by the terms of the charge. In *Re Brightlife Ltd* it was stated *obiter* that if there is clear language then automatic crystallisation can take place. Automatic crystallisation thus would mean that on the serving of the notice such as on our facts crystallisation would take place.

In *Re Brightlife Ltd* the court was referred to the House of Lords decision in *Governments Stock & Other Securities Investment Co. Ltd* v *Manila Railway Co. Ltd* [1897] AC 81, where it was stated that crystallisation was fixed by law and not by the agreement of the parties. That is, the only events that could bring about crystallisation are (a) winding up, (b) appointment of a receiver and (c) ceasing to carry on business. However in *Re Brightlife Ltd*, Hoffmann J stated that the *Governments Stock and Other Securities* case was about construction of the document. The court thus went on to state that there must not be any restriction on the freedom to contract of the parties to a floating charge. It could therefore be said here that crystallisation had occurred when the notice was served on the company.

Turning now to the question of whether the Commissioners of Customs and Excise can have priority over Flora in relation to the book debts, the position today has to be considered in the context of section 175(2)(b) of the Insolvency Act 1986. By that section, where assets of the company available for payment of general creditors are insufficient to meet them, preferential debts have priority over the claims of holders of any floating charge created by the company and would be paid accordingly. Even if the charge has been crystallised the chargeholder cannot claim that the charge is a fixed one as section 175 refers to the charge as being created as a floating charge. Preferential debts are identified in the Insolvency Act and include VAT and some other taxes payable to Customs and Excise. In the event of an adminstrative receiver being appointed by the debenture holder section 40 of the Insolvency Act 1986 states that the receiver has to pay off preferential creditors in priority to any charge that has been created as a floating charge even if it is claimed that automatic crystallisation has taken place.

In conclusion it must be noted that if the chargee here, Flora, was a holder of a fixed charge on the book debts then the security could be realised while ignoring preferential creditors.

QUESTION 3

Consider if the rejection by the Cork Committee of radical proposals for total abolition of floating charges was a mistake?

Commentary

The question requires a consideration of the Cork Committee's proposals concerning floating charges. It would also be necessary to express a view on why the Cork Committee did not accept the abolition of floating charges. Details of the Cork Committe's report are given in ch. 15 of *Cases and Materials on Company Law* by A. Hicks and S. H. Goo.

Suggested Answer

The floating charge which was developed particularly in the Victorian period was seen at that time and today as a very flexible way of providing a company with capital on such terms that would be helpful to the company and individual creditors.

The floating charge enables the company's current assets, which are 'floating assets', to be used in the ordinary course of its business. The creditor would be able to realise his security by causing the charge to crystallise. On crystallisation what would happen is that the charge fastens on whatever property is in existence at the time of crystallisation. Although a floating chargee being an equitable chargee has no right to possession of the charged property, the chargee could under the debenture deed take charge of the assets through a receiver appointed as a company's agent. The receiver would come under a duty to utilise the company's property and business to meet the obligation owed to the charger.

Having considered some characteristics of the floating charge it is evident that the company can be apparently in possession of assets of great value, so as to obtain credit from suppliers.

The other problem that has been often observed is that a receiver can be appointed at any time and this would fasten the charge on the assets.

Unsecured creditors also find that in many cases the floating charge holder obtains a charge on the company's entire undertaking which means that in the event of insolvency, the whole of the assets fall to be realised outside the winding up. There is also the concern here that by the time the receiver has dealt with the company's undertaking there would be nothing left for the unsecured creditors.

In the case of most businesses the assets will fall to be realised not by the liquidator but by the receiver. The receiver would retain goods for which the supplier has not been paid. The receiver and manager possess wide powers of management, and in certain cases it is found that the receiver disposes of parts of the business as a going concern.

The Cork Committee was faced with these criticisms but nevertheless decided to retain floating charges and at the same time provide safeguards. Before considering the safeguards the Committee proposed, it would be necessary to consider some of the strengths of floating charges. The floating charge is advantageous as it enables the secured lender, often a bank, to appoint an administrative receiver to preside over the virtual liquidation of all the company's free assets for the benefit of the secured creditor. The banks have often argued that the floating charge is essential to keep the free flow of finance to business. The Cork Committee was also impressed by the fact that in many instances the administrative receiver in realising the assets of a company sells off businesses as a going concern rather than on a break-up basis.

Turning now to the safeguards introduced by the Cork Committee in relation to floating charges. Section 245 of the Insolvency Act 1986 which invalidates a floating charge except to the extent of the value of so much of the consideration for the creation of the charge. There is the relevant time period during which the charge has to be created which in the case of connected persons is a period of two years ending with the onset of insolvency and in the case of any other person 12 months ending with the onset of insolvency. In the case of non-connected persons the charge could by section 245(4) only be set aside if the company was unable to pay its debts. Further under section 239 of the Insolvency Act 1986 a floating charge could be set aside on the grounds that it was a preference, that is, to prefer one creditor over the others.

The Cork Committee also decided, and this was implemented, to introduce the concept of an 'administrative receiver' which is a receiver appointed by a creditor with a charge over all the company's assets or a substantial part of the assets. The Insolvency Act 1986 then goes on to deal with the powers of the administrative receiver so as to encourage management of the business with a view of improving the fortunes of the company. Also the creditor under a debenture who can appoint an administrative receiver can object to the appointment of an administrator.

The Cork Committee was concerned about automatic crystallisation. The Committee concluded that the possibility of crystallisation without the appointment of a receiver puts at risk persons dealing with a company, as the company's power of disposition ceases. Further the Committee also concluded that it was highly inconvenient if the floating charge was crystallised against the wishes of the parties. This would happen when there is a technical default.

The Committee then proceeded to recommend that the circumstances in which a charge will crystallise should be specified by statute and limited to the following, that is, on the commencement of a winding up, on appointment of an administrator, or the appointment of a receiver under any other floating charge on any assets or property of the company.

The recommendations were not implemented by the Insolvency Act 1986. In conclusion it may be said that it would not be practical to abolish floating charges in view of their practical benefits to companies. The concerns of unsecured creditors were by and large dealt with by the Committee's recommendations and the implementation of the Insolvency Act. In respect of automatic crystallisation, the Insolvency Act 1986, it could be said, did not go far enough. However, if section 100 of the Companies Act 1989 is brought into force it will insert a new section 410 into the Companies Act 1985 giving the Secretary of State power to make regulations requiring notice to be given to the registrar of companies of any event which crystallises a registered floating charge. No such regulations have yet been made.

10 Shares

INTRODUCTION

A student coming to deal with this area should be first of all aware of the legal nature of shares. In *Borland's Trustee* v *Steel Brothers & Co. Ltd* [1901] 1 Ch 279, a share was identified as an interest of a shareholder in the company measured by a sum of money for the purpose of liability in the first place and of interest in the second. The court had also referred to the share as being subject to the section 14 contract. The contract contained in the articles of association is one of the original incidents of the share.

It would be also necessary to consider the method of transfer of shares and particularly the role of directors. The other aspect that a student should be familiar with is rights attaching to shares particularly as to voting and dividends. Students should read particularly ch. 14 and 15 of *Gower's Principles of Modern Company Law*, 15th ed., *Cases and Materials on Company Law* by Andrew Hicks and S.H. Goo has an excellent collection of relevant materials including an extract from Robert Pennington's article (1989) 10 Co Law 140 on whether shares in companies can be defined.

QUESTION 1

John, David and Sara are shareholders and directors of We-will Ltd, a company specialising in home renovation. John was a majority shareholder and for some years attempted to learn home renovation. One day he suffered an electric shock from which he died. His widow, Dolly, wanted, as executrix of his estate, to have John's shares purchased by the others. The company's articles provided for surviving directors to buy the shares of a deceased at a valuation certified as 'fair' by the auditor, acting as an expert. The company had been making losses over the few years that John was trying to make the business work. Advise Dolly on the possible way in which a valuation could proceed and whether any application could be made to court to challenge a valuation.

Suggested Answer

The auditor here can proceed on the basis of considering the shareholding as a majority holding and that the purchaser of the shares would get a controlling interest. In this way the valuation would proceed on the basis of a premium. The Court of Appeal in *Dean* v *Prince* [1954] Ch 409 stated that the shareholding in a company should be valued on an equal basis. To Denning LJ the proper approach would be to consider the worth of the business itself and then to value the number of shares as a proportion of the value of the business.

The other possibility for valuaton is treating the business as a going concern. The question that has to be addressed here is whether the business is relatively successful. The facts suggest that John had been learning the business and this could show that the company may not being doing well. If the auditor finds here that the company is making losses then it may be wound up. On such evidence the shares cannot be valued with the company being treated as a going concern. If the company is not going to be treated as a going concern, the only way to make the valuation is to deal with the assets. The auditor could proceed on the basis of a buyer making an offer for the entire business, that is, the stock in trade, and the premises if there is any freehold property. On the facts here it is not clear what type of premises the business is operating from. If they are only leasehold premises there is still the issue of whether the lease is assignable.

When it comes to the valuation of the assets what has to be considered is whether the assets could be valued on a break-up basis. If the business has not been doing well, then a purchaser would want to purchase plant and machinery not on a book value of assets but on the value that could be obtained on an auction. A valuer would therefore be required to value the assets on a loss basis if the company is making losses.

If Dolly, as executrix, can find a buyer who would be interested in buying John's shares then it could be argued that such a purchaser could come into the business and have it reorganised having removed the other directors.

The auditor, it can be argued, should consider a valuation on the basis of such a purchaser of shares. In *Dean* v *Prince* the Court of Appeal went on to state that considering the possibility of a special purchaser as the basis of a valuation was not correct as the other directors are working directors and would want to continue with the company. The Court of Appeal stated that it would be unfair to get the other directors to pay a price for the shares on the basis of being turned out.

Dolly should be advised here that whatever basis the auditor should adopt in the valuation a court would only interfere if the auditor has proceeded on a wrong principle.

On the point of the controlling interest John's shares may carry, the law does not provide an easy answer. In private companies a controlling interest would be helpful as controlling shareholders can appoint themselves to the board. This would mean also that directors who are shareholders would be able to receive remuneration as directors as opposed to dividends.

QUESTION 2

Shares confer a bundle of rights. Discuss.

Commentary

The question requires a consideration of the different rights associated with shares. It would be necessary to emphasise particularly here the issue of the articles of association and how the rights associated with shares are very different from other types of property rights.

Suggested Answer

When considering the passage it must be first borne in mind that membership of a company limited by shares means an undertaking to contribute towards the capital of the company by the member. At the same time, whether it is a small private company or a larger public company, the articles of association and the memorandum determine the rights of the member. The reference in the question to the 'bundle of rights' would seem to cover these aspects.

It would be necessary to examine both aspects, that is, the undertaking to contribute to the capital and the role of the articles and memorandum.

A share provides a unit for measuring a member's interest in the company. The Companies Act 1985 by section 2(5)(a) requires a sum of money to be assigned as the nominal value of a share. This is the minimum value that a company must demand to receive as contributed capital in exchange for the share.

A shareholder could undertake to contribute more for shares than their nominal value. This would result in the excess being termed as a share premium. The premium would have to be accounted for as part of the share premium account. The memorandum would state the total nominal value of the shares a company may allot to the members. The paid-up share capital of a company is the amount actually contributed to its share capital.

In the event of the company being wound up when it is solvent then the capital contributed by the members is returned to them. On the other hand if the company is insolvent then all the assets acquired with the members' contributed capital will have to be used to pay the company's debts and nothing will be returned to the members.

The nominal value of the shares held by a member of a company measures the member's liability to contribute capital to the company. In return the member through the size of the shareholding would through the votes attached to the shares influence decision making when voting in general meeting.

A member would also be entitled to participate when the company makes a distribution of its property to its members. This could occur in winding up if there is a surplus after paying all of its creditors and repaying its contributed capital. Members would also be entitled to a distribution of profits if there are annual profits and the distribution would be termed a dividend. Turning now to the aspect of the membership rights attaching to the shares by virtue of the articles. In respect of the payment of dividends, by the articles, for instance by Table A, article 102, the directors would recommend the dividends and this would be approved by the members. Table A, article 104, provides that each member would receive a dividend in proportion to the nominal value of the shares held, or the amount paid up if they are partly paid up. By the articles the member's rights would depend on the specification of the rights at the time of allotment of shares. In most cases we would be concerned with ordinary shares. There is no specific definition in the Companies Act 1985 of what an ordinary share is but in the case of *Norman* v *Norman* (1990) 19 NSWLR 314 it was stated that the term meant a share other than a preference share. A preference share would be advantageous to a member as the preference shareholder would be entitled to an annual dividend of a fixed amount per share and would be paid in priority to any dividend payments to other members. When dealing with the rights of the preference shareholders any statement of the entitlement to an annual dividend and a share of surplus assets in winding up must be construed as defining those rights exhaustively.

The articles of association would also be important in respect of voting at meetings of shareholders. The general principle is that every member of the company has a right to vote at a general meeting of the company's members. Normally each individual member has one vote which is to be exercised by a show of hands. Companies normally allow for members present at meetings to have a number of votes proportional to the number of shares. However, this must be exercised only when voting is by polls. In *Northern Counties Securities Ltd* v *Jackson & Steeple Ltd* [1974] 1 WLR 1133, the court was not prepared to grant an order of specific performance to compel members to vote in a particular way. The Companies Act 1985 leaves it to the company to specify whether members are to have weighted voting rights. However, most articles follow article 54 of Table A by stating that each shareholder would have one vote on a show of hands and each share would have one vote on a poll. The vote by show of hands highlights the principle of presumption of equality between shareholders. This principle was carried a step further by the Companies Act of 1980 which implemented the second Company Law Directive. This Directive requires every member State to ensure equal treatment to all shareholders who are in the same position. Section 80 of the 1985 Companies Act, to which section 80A was added by the 1989 Act, provides that directors shall not exercise any power of the company to allot shares in the company or rights to subscribe for or convert into shares unless they are authorised by the company in general meeting or the company's articles. Further by sections 89 to 96 there are pre-emptive rights. In summary what these provisions do is to ensure that equity securities are not allotted to any person unless the company has first offered on the same or more favourable terms, to each person who holds relevant shares or relevant employee shares, a proportion of those equity securities which is as nearly as practicable equal to his existing proportion of the nominal value of the aggregate holdings of the relevant securities.

QUESTION 3

(a)   A plc was registered as a public limited company and commenced business. It now has a share capital of 30,000 £1 shares fully paid. This was after the company had purchased some of its own shares last year. The articles are in the form of the 1985 Table A.

The directors are planning to hold a meeting of the board where they propose to carry out the following allotments:

(i)   10,000 £1 shares to Joe on the basis of 10 pence per share as paid up.

(ii)   5,000 £1 shares to Charles in return for Charles agreeing to provide free accounting services to a friend of one of the directors of A plc.

(iii)   7,000 £1 participating preference shares to David at £2 per share.

Advise the directors.

(b)   Gems Ltd is a company specialising in importing diamonds from a Far Eastern country. The articles are in the form of Table A with an additional article which states that 'Directors can refuse to register any transfer they do not approve of'.

In March of 1999 Jade, a member of Gems Ltd decided to sell her shares to Mon with the sale price being paid within two months of sale. The sale transfer form was lodged by Mon in April 1999. In July the secretary of the company sent a letter to Mon informing him that his application was rejected as Mon was politically opposed to the gems trade with the Far Eastern State and would not be a suitable member of the company. Advise Jade who states that Mon has failed to pay for the shares.

Commentary

The first part of the question deals with the issues of re-registration of a public limited company as a private limited company. There is also the need to consider the validity of the allotment of the shares. The second part deals with directors' powers in dealing with share transfers and particularly the effects of the directors' refusal to register on the contract of sale.

Suggested Answer

(a)   The first issue to be considered here would be the need for A plc to re-register as a private company.

Re-registration as a Private Company

By section 117 of the 1985 Companies Act a company which is registered as a public company on its original incorporation cannot do any business or exercise any borrowing powers unless the registrar of companies has issued it with a certificate to commence business or it is re-registered as a private company. This is necessary here as being a public limited company it must have an authorised capital at least of £50,000 this being the current requirement under section 118 of the Companies Act. The other alternative for the directors would be to issue further shares so as to increase the capital to the minimum authorised capital of £50,000 as set out in section 118 of the Companies Act 1985.

Issuing Further Shares to Bring the Capital to £50,000

The directors have to be advised that by section 80 of the 1985 Companies Act there must be authority under the articles of the company or by the company in general meeting for the directors to allot shares. Assuming that there is the necessary authority, then the directors must offer the shares that are to be issued on a pre-emptive basis by section 89 of the Companies Act 1985. This would mean that the company must not allot shares on any terms to a person unless it has made an offer to each person who holds the company's equity shares on the same or more favourable terms a proportion of those securities which is as nearly as practicable equal to the proportion in nominal value held by him of the aggregate of relevant shares and relevant employee shares. There is also a need to observe that by section 95 of the 1985 Companies Act the directors of a company can be authorised for purposes of section 80 either by the articles or by a special resolution to disapply the pre-emption rights. Turning now to the issues relating to the issue of the shares to the particular individuals.

10,000 £1 Shares to Joe

The allotment of shares is not going to be valid as far as Joe is concerned as by section 101 a public company cannot allot shares except as paid up at least as to a quarter of their nominal value. The position here is that, by section 101(4), Joe will be liable to pay the company the minimum amount which should have been received in respect of the share under subsection (1) (less the value of any consideration actually applied in payment up to any extent of the share and a premium on it).

5,000 £1 Shares to Charles

The issue of shares to Charles is in contravention of section 100 of the Companies Act 1985 which prohibits the issue of shares at a discount.

The section 100 provision is a statutory version of the common law rule confirmed by the House of Lords in *Ooregum Gold Mining Co. of India Ltd* v *Roper* [1892] AC 125. In that case Lord Halsbury LC stated that the nature of an agreement to take a share in a limited company is that it is an agreement to become liable to pay the amount for which the share has been created.

The company also, following from this, cannot give away its shares, treating them as fully paid up though it has not received anything. This would also be covered by the wording of section 100.

The consequence of this allotment contravening section 100 is that Charles would be liable here to pay the amount of the discount, that is, the sum of £5,000, and by section 107 of the Companies Act 1985 to pay interest at 5 per cent a year.

7,000 £1 Participating Preference Shares

Here the directors would have to ensure that the amount exceeding the nominal value is treated separately from the nominal value. This would mean that the balance sheet of the company would have to represent the share premium as a subheading. Section 130 of the 1985 Companies Act deals with the setting up of the 'share premium account'. The legislative policy here is that the share premium account has to be treated in the same way as the share capital and the rules of capital preservation also apply to the share premium account.

(b)   The first issue that has to be considered here is the lodging of the share transfer form with the company and the company's obligations. By section 185 of the Companies Act 1985, every company must within two months after the date on which a transfer of any shares is lodged be in a position to complete and have share certificates ready for delivery.

Jade, the transferor, can at this stage apply for a court order directing the company and any officer to make good the default.

The next issue that has to be considered is whether the directors exercised the power under the articles validly. In the Court of Appeal decision of *Re Smith & Fawcett Ltd* [1942] Ch 304, it was held that articles of association such as the one here can confer a discretion on directors which must be exercised bona fide in the interests of the company. In our particular case it would appear that the directors are in a position to take into account the company's business and whether the tranferee's attitude towards the business would be detrimental to the company. It is a matter on which the court cannot impose its views.

The other question that has to be considered here is the procedure for refusing to register. In *Tett* v *Phoenix Property and Investment Co. Ltd* [1984] BCLC 149, it was held that a positive resolution not to register must be taken at a properly convened board meeting. Also in *Re Swaledale Cleaners Ltd* [1968] 1 WLR 1710, it was held that the directors' power to refuse to register had to be exercised within the statutory time period for consideration of the transfer. Here it would be the two-month period now set out in section 185 of the 1985 Companies Act. Section 183(5) requires the company to send a notice to the transferee within two months of lodgment of a transfer of a refusal to register it.

If the refusal of the directors to register is valid, then the contract of sale between Jade and Mon would be unenforceable. This is the case as it would be an implied term of the contract that the transfer would have to take effect in accordance with the articles. If the directors' refusal is invalid then Jade has to take steps to compel registration of Mon as a shareholder otherwise she would be liable for non-delivery when completion is due.

QUESTION 4

Mike was one of the five directors of a property development company, Basildon Development Ltd. The company's articles included article 73(b) which provided that a director shall vacate his office if requested in writing by all his co-directors to resign. Following the company's incorporation relations between the directors were harmonious till Mike believed that the chairman of the board of the company had sold one of the company's properties to a friend at an undervalue.

When Mike asked to have access to various accounts and documents this was not complied with. The company then passed a resolution which was passed with the shareholding of the other directors, ratifying a breach of duties. Mike, has now received a notice signed by the other directors requiring him to resign pursuant to article 73(b).

Advise Mike who wants to bring a personal action to prevent his removal from the board. He wants also to bring a derivative action on behalf of the company against the chairman of the board for the loss suffered by the company.

Commentary

The question requires the consideration of the directors' duties in relation to the exercise of their powers under the articles particularly in relation to the resignation of a director. On the issue of the derivative action it is crucial to identify what is meant by 'fraud on the minority' in relation to the disposal of the company's property at an undervalue.

Suggested Answer

We would begin by considering the exercise by the directors of the power under article 73(b) of the company's articles. The power of the directors under article 73(b) has to be exercised like any other power conferred on the directors. This would mean that it has to be in the interests of the company.

In the circumstances this would mean that each director concurring in the expulsion must act in accordance with what he believes to be the interests of the company. The Privy Council in *Lee* v *Chou Wen Hsien* [1984] 1 WLR 1202 dealt with a similar article and confirmed that the directors have to act bona fide in the interests of the company.

The difficulty here on our facts is that the chairman may not be acting in good faith and would be concerned with his own self-interest. In the *Lee* case the Privy Council was not prepared to permit the notice to a director requiring his resignation to be invalid merely because of the lack of bona fides on the part of the director.

The Privy Council was concerned with the practical issue of ensuring that the article there was interpreted in the business sense. Therefore in the case of the present article anyone considering its exercise by the directors would expect the wording to be adhered to strictly. The Privy Council in the *Lee* case was prepared to hold that the office of the director was vacated on the occurrence of the event set out in the articles.

It may be argued by the company that if an injunction was granted the management of the company would be held up pending the resolution of the dispute. It may be suggested that the decision of the Privy Council is not surprising in view of there being a clear case of lack of good faith on the part of one of the directors. It is likely that the English courts would follow the Privy Council decision. The decision of the Privy Council could be said to reflect the view of the courts that members of the board should be able to decide for themselves as to whether they can work with one another and if there is a lack of confidence that a director should be removed.

In the circumstances Mike must be advised that it is not going to be possible for an injunction to be obtained to restrain the board from requiring him to resign.

Turning now to the company's decision to ratify in general meeting the breach of fiduciary duties by the chairman.

Mike should be advised that any fiduciary duty that is owed by the directors is owed to the company and, following *Foss* v *Harbottle* (1843) 2 Hare 461 the proper plaintiff is the company.

The general meeting has now decided that no action would be taken against the chairman. The rule in *Foss* v *Harbottle* maintains the importance of majority rule. If Mike wants to bring an action then it has to be a derivative action. The first issue that has to be decided is whether there is a 'fraud'. In considering the authorities it would appear that only where the wrongdoers appropriate corporate assets and opportunities would there be fraud. In *Pavlides* v *Jensen* [1956] Ch 565, the court held that mere negligence was not a fraud on the minority.

In *Pavlides* the plaintiff, a minority shareholder, brought a derivative action against the directors and the company alleging that they had been negligent in selling the company's mine at an undervalue. The defendants objected to the action on the basis that the plaintiff had no right. The court agreed with that contention since there were no allegations of the appropriation of corporate assets. If there is negligence or error of judgment then it was held that the general meeting can vote on whether proceedings should be taken.

In the later case of *Daniels* v *Daniels* [1978] Ch 406, the company had sold an asset at a gross undervalue. The purchaser of the asset who profited later by selling the asset at a profit was a director of the company. The minority shareholder succeeded in bringing a derivative action. The court, following *Menier* v *Hooper's Telegraph Works* (1874) LR 9 Ch App 350, concluded that whenever directors use their powers intentionally or unintentionally fraudulently or negligently in a manner which benefits themselves at the expense of the company, then a minority shareholder would have satisfied the principles in the same way as a 'fraud on the minority'.

In our case there is no evidence of the director, the chairman, benefiting personally from the transaction. *Daniels* v *Daniels* distinguished *Pavlides* v *Jensen* as in the *Pavlides* case there was gross negligence without personal profiting. It is immaterial that the chairman and other directors who may have been in control at the general meeting may not be acting in the interests of the company. What is important to note here is that at the general meeting the shareholder, even if a director, can vote in his own self-interest. In *North-West Transportation Co. Ltd* v *Beatty* (1887) 12 App Cas 589, the Privy Council held that although a director is precluded from dealing on behalf of the company with himself and from entering into engagements in which he has a conflicting personal interest, the director can, as a member, vote in his own interest to affirm such an act so long as it is not illegal or fraudulent or oppressive.

However, in *Estmanco (Kilner House) Ltd* v *Greater London Council* [1982] 1 WLR 2, Megarry V-C expressed the view that fraud on the minority is not confined to common law fraud. His lordship proceeded on the basis that a fraud can also be established when considering the exercise of the voting power. The test that was proposed was to consider if the voting was in the interest of the company. Megarry V-C reviewed the authorities and concluded that a derivative action can be brought if there is a misuse of power. However, the judgment of Megarry V-C is inconsistent with the Privy Council decision of *North-West Transportation Co. Ltd* v *Beatty*.

Mike would have to be advised here that a derivative action cannot be based on establishing fraud on a power.

11 Directors' Duties, Appointment and Removal

INTRODUCTION

This chapter is concerned with the directors' trustee-like obligations, which is an extremely wide-ranging area. It would be useful here to consider L.S. Sealy's article 'The director as trustee' [1967] CLJ 83.

There is a need then to consider appointment of directors pursuant to articles. The effect of the articles on other matters such as removal and remuneration is also important. The consequences of directors' duties being owed to the company and the enforcement of these duties would also require one to consider the effects here of the rule in *Foss* v *Harbottle* which we have already considered.

In more recent years disqualification of directors has been growing in importance. There is now the Company Directors Disqualification Act 1986. There is a comprehensive coverage of the position of directors in ch. 11 of *Cases and Materials on Company Law* by Andrew Hicks and S.H. Goo. The chapter is also useful on material concerning the Report of the Committee on the Financial Aspects of Corporate Governance (the Cadbury Report).

QUESTION 1

'I think it is important to emphasise that what I am asked to consider is the alleged fiduciary duty of directors to current shareholders as sellers of their shares. This must not be confused with their duty to consider the interests of shareholders in the discharge of their duty to the company. What is in the interests of current shareholders who are sellers of their shares may not necessarily coincide with what is in the interests of the company. The creation of parallel duties could lead to a conflict. Directors have but one master, the company.' Lord Cullen in *Dawson International plc* v *Coats Patons plc* (1989). Discuss.

Commentary

The question requires consideration of the various interests directors have to consider when dealing with a takeover bid. The answer would have to deal with the meaning of 'interests of the company' and the conflict directors find themselves in when dealing with a takeover bid.

Suggested Answer

The passage quoted refers to the issue of directors' duties in relation to recommending whether shareholders should accept a takeover bid. The passage by Lord Cullen also raises what is meant by 'interests of members' when exploring the duties of directors. It is proposed to deal with these issues first by considering the duties of directors in relation to a takeover bid and then to proceed to consider the position in relation to shareholders' rights particularly in relation to provisions of the articles and their rights not to have their interests unfairly prejudiced. It could be suggested here that it is probably shareholders enforcing rights under the articles that has resulted in the view that directors owe a duty to current shareholders in relation to the sale of their shares.

Directors generally owe duties to the company. These duties involve not only the fiduciary duty implied by equity but also at common law to act in the interests of the company. As acknowledged by Lord Cullen in the *Dawson* case, the fiduciary duties spring from directors being agents of the company and today, by section 309 of the Companies Act 1985, include the interests of employees. On the issue of the meaning of interests of members Megarry J in *Gaiman* v *National Association for Mental Health* [1977] Ch 317, stated that the company is an artificial legal entity and that the interests of members is going to be the present and future members. This duty of acting in the interests of the company is treated as being the commercial interests of members thus maximimising their investment.

The difficulty arises in those cases where directors utilise their powers to act in the interests of the company but for improper purposes. In *Hogg* v *Cramphorn Ltd* [1967] Ch 254, the directors wanted to allot shares so as to prevent a takeover in the honest belief that the takeover would not be in the interests of the company. The Chancery Division held that it was irrelevant that the directors had acted in good faith, as the power to issue shares here was used by the directors to manipulate the voting position so that their supporters would be in control. It could be seen here that directors did not owe any duty towards individual shareholders. The fact that directors can take into account the interests of existing shareholders in the discharge of their duty should not be confused with a fiduciary duty towards these members in the disposal of their shares.

What has to be considered next is the significance of the Court of Appeal decision in *Heron International Ltd* v *Lord Grade* [1983] BCLC 244. Here there was a takeover bid for the Associated Communications Corporation plc of which Lord Grade was chairman and chief executive. Lord Grade and his fellow directors agreed to transfer their own shares to the bidder but Heron International Ltd had acquired shares in the company and wished to launch a rival bid at a higher price. The problem here was that if the transfers of the directors' shares had gone through it would give the first bidder a majority of the votes in the company and Heron's bid would inevitably fail.

The Court of Appeal held that the duty to determine which person shall acquire and be registered as the holder of shares is a fiduciary power which must be exercised in the interests of the company and in the interests of the shareholders of the company. The court also went further to state that if there are two bidders then interests of the current shareholders should be taken into account. The decision in the *Heron* case involved article 29 of the articles of association which gave directors the power to decide who should be the purchaser and transferee when any shareholder desired to sell his shares. It could be argued that the case was more about enforcement of rights under the articles than the existence of a fiduciary duty towards current shareholders. In the *Dawson International* case Lord Cullen concluded that the *Heron* case was precisely about the duty of directors on the construction of the articles. It is also possible to state here that if directors do not consider particular interests of the current shareholders, there could be a petition under section 459 of the Companies Act 1985 on the basis that it was unfairly prejudicial to the interests of current members. However, all this is not evidence of any positive duty of directors towards shareholders.

Although directors may not owe a particular fidicuary duty to current shareholders, it must also be observed that directors can have liability in negligence at common law when recommending or not recommending a bid. Lord Cullen had further stated in the *Dawson International* case that directors have to give advice to current shareholders in good faith if they do take on such a function, and they must not deliberately mislead members.

All this would still not show any basis of a specific fiduciary duty as any remedies must be specifically enforced by individual shareholders. Lord Cullen in the *Dawson International* case was prepared to treat the potential liability based on general principles of law as being a so-called secondary fiduciary duty to the shareholders.

In conclusion it may be stated that the *Dawson International* decision follows the traditional principles of company law in holding that directors' fiduciary duty is to act in the long-term interests of all shareholders. It is, however, regretted that the law has not been able to identify a more limited specific fiduciary duty to current shareholders in the event of a takeover bid, particularly since what could happen to a company after a takeover may be beyond the control of the existing directors. In the final analysis it could be stated that the court was avoiding a possible conflict if parallel duties as suggested by Lord Cullen are recognised.

QUESTION 2

Zouk Ltd (the company) is a company that operates a disco and restaurant. Danny, the managing director of the company in early 1999 had met a Bruce Tan who had been prepared to contract with Zouk Ltd to provide singers and bands from Hong Kong, as there was a demand amongst the mainly Chinese patrons of the company. The company had entered into a contract with Bruce Tan.

In mid-2000 Danny resigned as managing director and now has established a company whose business activities include a karaoke lounge in Soho, London and has contracted with Bruce Tan to use bands and singers that would normally be sent to the company, Zouk Ltd. The directors of the company want to be advised if there is any cause of action against Danny. The band and singers have a good reputation and can increase Zouk Ltd's profits.

Commentary

The question requires particular consideration of the decision of Hutchinson J in *Island Export Finance Ltd* v *Umunna* [1986] BCLC 460. The case is an endorsement of the corporate opportunity doctrine.

In dealing with the question it would be necessary to consider the orthodox view in dealing with fiduciary duties.

Suggested Answer

The directors of the company would have to be advised here that Danny as a director starts off owing a fiduciary duty. In *Regal (Hastings) Ltd* v *Gulliver* [1967] 2 AC 134, the House of Lords held that directors are not allowed to make a profit out of their position as directors. The rule is a strict one to the effect that where directors have obtained a benefit only by reason of the fact that they are directors and in the course of the execution of their office, they are accountable for any profits which they have made.

The directors here would have to be advised that on our facts Danny has set out to exploit the opportunity after resigning from the company. It would be necessary at this stage to deal with the Canadian decision of *Canadian Aero Service Ltd* v *O'Malley* (1973) 40 DLR (3d) 371. The Supreme Court of Canada accepted the principle that the case law in Canada and other jurisdictions established that fiduciary duties of directors and senior officers disqualify them from usurping for themselves or diverting to another person or company with whom they are associated a maturing business opportunity which the company is pursuing.

In *Canadian Aero Service Ltd* v *O'Malley* two defendants had for some years been working towards a detailed and complex project which had almost come to fruition of which they had a particular knowledge and which plainly they planned while still employed by the company. The Supreme Court held that the defendants would not have acquired the knowledge of it were it not for their work done for the company.

On the facts it is not very clear in what circumstances Danny left the employment of the company. However, at this stage, the fact that Danny has approached Bruce Tan to divert singers and bands to Danny's establishment, would suggest that there is a possibility of Danny resigning to utilise the opportunity. In *Island Export Finance Ltd* v *Umunna*, Hutchinson J was prepared to accept the doctrine in the *Canadian Aero Service* case. His lordship held that the decision of the Supreme Court was consistent with principles laid down in the line of authorities of which *Regal (Hastings) Ltd* is an example.

In the light of the decision in *Island Export Finance* it is relevant to note that the court would not be prepared to accept the distinction, that *Regal Hastings* would not be applicable in instances where the fiduciary relationship has come to an end.

The directors here could also rely on the decision of Roskill J in *Industrial Development Consultants Ltd* v *Cooley* [1972] 1 WLR 443. Here the defendant had left the employment of the plaintiffs and obtained the benefit of a contract. This was the result of work which he did while still the plaintiffs' managing director. The court held that the defendant held the contract as a constructive trustee for the plaintiffs.

In the *Island Export Finance* case the court was not prepared to accept the submission of the defendants that the *Cooley* decision was a case on breach of duty relating to actions of the defendant while still employed.

The other factor that has to be considered here is the principles relating to contracts of restraint of trade, the general position being that in the absence of a restraint of trade clause Danny here should be free to compete with the former employers.

In the *Canadian Aero Service* case it was the view of Laskin J that whenever directors exploit for their own or a new employer's benefit information which while they may have come by it solely because of their position as directors they would be accountable. Here, Danny had represented the company when the opportunity was to be exploited.

By contrast in the *Island Export* case, the court found that the defendant had not resigned to exploit an opportunity. Also the business opportunity the defendant in the *Island Export* case was pursuing was one that had not fully matured when he left his employment.

After the decision in *Island Export Finance Ltd*, in *Balston Ltd* v *Headlines Filters Ltd* [1990] FSR 385, Falconer J followed Hutchinson J in stating that a former director can start a competing business even though the intention to commence business was formed prior to the resignation so long as there was no maturing business opportunity which was being usurped.

In conclusion it can be stated that the directors would have a good prospect of succeeding against Danny on the basis of his fiduciary duties.

The appropriate remedy would be the imposition of a constructive trust. In the circumstances he would be required to account for profits which he had obtained from the diversion of the business.

QUESTION 3

'Directors are not really trustees. They are businessmen and should be recognised as such.' Discuss this statement in the context of directors' fiduciary duties. Do you think that directors should today be subject to trustee-like obligations?

Commentary

The question requires first a consideration of the overriding equitable obligation of directors and developments in this area in more recent years. It is important for the purposes of the question to deal with whether directors should be subject to trustee-like obligations.

Suggested Answer

The existence of the fiduciary obligations of directors has been traced, for instance, by L.S. Sealy in his article 'The director as trustee' [1967] CLJ 83 as being due to early directors being trustees of the company's assets under a deed of settlement. However, whatever the origins of the comparison of directors with trustees it came to be established that directors belong to the category which, in the judgment of Bowen LJ in *Imperial Hydropathic Hotel Co., Blackpool* v *Hampson* (1882) 23 ChD 1, is similar to trustees, or managing partners of the company. What can be said is that directors' fiduciary duties have evolved by analogy to trustees.

In *Aberdeen Railway Co.* v *Blaikie Bros* [1843–60] All ER 249, Lord Cranworth LC referred to a director being an agent of the company who would come under a duty to ensure that he does not enter into engagements in which he had a personal interest conflicting with the interests of persons he is bound to protect.

In the *Blaikie* case the matter that had come before a court concerned a director of a company who was a partner of a firm which was selling chairs to the company. To Lord Cranworth, when the director was acting in his capacity as a director representing the company, he was also contracting on behalf of the firm. The court found that since the function of the director was to obtain the chairs at the lowest cost the existence of a personal interest would be entirely in the opposite direction, that is, to induce him to fix the price as high as possible.

The House of Lords was not prepared to exempt directors from the principles of there being no conflict of duty and personal interest. To the House of Lords the trustee-like obligation was justifiable as a person acting as manager of a mercantile or trading business for the benefit of others is in no different position from that of a trustee employed in selling land.

The decision in *Aberdeen Railway Co.* v *Blaikie Bros.* thus confirmed the application of the rule in *Keech* v *Sandford* (1726) 25 ER 223 as to directors in exactly the same way as it would apply to trustees. That is the 'self-dealing' rule whereby the company can set aside a transaction or get a director to account irrespective of the fairness of the transaction. The application of the trustee-like obligation can sometimes lead to harshness. A leading case here is *Regal (Hastings) Ltd* v *Gulliver* [1967] 2 AC 134. Here the House of Lords held that directors who had subscribed for shares with the consent of the board were liable to account to the company. This was the case notwithstanding that the company had no financial resources itself to subscribe for the shares. The majority of the House of Lords concluded that a person occupying a fiduciary relationship should not make a profit from his fiduciary position and this inflexible rule had to apply notwithstanding that it would be unjust in the given circumstances.

At the Court of Appeal stage Lord Greene was not prepared to impose an obligation on the directors to account as the only way they could secure the benefit for the company was by putting up the money to acquire the shares themselves.

From the above discussion it would appear that it is not correct in principle to continue to subject directors to trustee-like obligations when they serve a wide variety of functions, the most important function often being their entrepreneurial skills. There is also the other practical problem where directors hold multi-directorships and can also be involved as directors in subsidiary and associated companies.

John Lowry in (1994) 45 NILQ 1 observed that because English law has viewed directors' duties from a multiplicity of liability models, such as the trustee concept, the principal–agent and employer–employee relationship, at times a restrictive and blinkered focus occurs based on particular legal states or capacity.

It could be suggested that what is required is still some recognition of a fiduciary duty in view of the responsibility that directors take in dealing with the company's affairs. Also if directors are involved in companies as businessmen we should be able to be sure that the interest of the company is not sacrificed. In these circumstances what is required is a more flexible approach as opposed to the inflexible approach in the earlier cases.

The alternative approach is sometimes referred to as the 'corporate opportunities doctrine'. Basically what the court considers here is whether some opportunity was actually pursued by the company. Also if the company had an opportunity to consider a possible investment which is offered to the company, then if a director chooses to pursue the matter there should not be an obligation to account.

Two decisions at first instance, namely, *Island Export Finance Ltd* v *Umunna* [1986] BCLC 460 and *Balston Ltd* v *Headlines Filters Ltd* [1990] FSR 385, would at the present show the acceptance of the more flexible approach.

In *Balston*, the defendant had been an employee–director of the company for some 17 years. Although the defendant had prior to his resignation leased business premises but had not decided on what business, after the defendant's resignation one of the company's customers approached him to supply goods when the company discontinued its supply.

The court held here that when the defendant took up the opportunity the company was not involved in any active pursuance of a business opportunity. In conclusion it can be argued that English law should continue the more flexible approach taken in the recent cases as opposed to what has developed in the last two centuries. One is here reminded of the statement in the 1992 consultation paper entitled *Fiduciary Duties and Regulatory Rules*, where it was stated 'this area of the law is highly complex, poorly delimited and in a state of flux'.

QUESTION 4

John and Jane are directors of A Ltd and own between them 65 per cent of the shares. There are seven other shareholders who take little or no part in the running of the company. Both John and Jane are also directors of B Ltd which is a company like A Ltd that deals with the development of food and entertainment establishments.

B Ltd went into creditors' voluntary winding up and there is a substanital deficit such that creditors expect no more than 10 pence in the pound. B Ltd had become insolvent mainly as a result of many speculative investments in attempting to develop food and entertainment establishments. A Ltd was also run by John and Jane on the basis of the same speculative policies and the company has suffered losses resulting in the company not being able to pay dividends for a period of time. John and Jane had also in 1999 and 2000 made considerable donations amounting to £100,000 to various charities.

The minority shareholders of A Ltd have discovered that John and Jane in 2000 had utilised their private funds in purchasing a property in South London for £100,000. At the material time A Ltd and B Ltd did not have the funds to purchase the property.

Recently the local authority has given planning permission for the site to be developed into a restaurant and both John and Jane are planning to sell the property for £500,000.

Advise the liquidator of B Ltd and the minority shareholders of A Ltd. Advise on the basis of the common law ignoring remedies under section 459 of the Companies Act 1985 and section 122(1)(g) of the Insolvency Act 1986.

Commentary

The question requires not only consideration of the equitable obligations of directors, but also aspects of the derivative action. There is also a need to consider the liquidator's rights against the directors. Of particular interest in this question is the position of the directors in relation to both companies in respect of any duty to account. It would be necessary to consider the earlier chapter on derivative actions. Again a question that can straddle many areas.

Suggested Answer

It would be convenient to consider first the minority shareholders' rights if any in relation to A Ltd.

Advice to Minority Shareholder of A Ltd

John and Jane as directors of A Ltd owe fiduciary duties to the company. In *Percival* v *Wright* [1902] 2 Ch 421, it was held that directors owe duties generally to the company and only in exceptional circumstances, for instance, in a takeover, do they owe duties to individual members.

It would follow that if there is any breach of fiduciary duties the proper plaintiff should be the company. The only way in which a member is going to be able to bring proceedings is using the name of the company. The derivative action is a procedure whereby although the claim is brought on behalf of the company it is brought in the name of the shareholders. It would be useful first to consider whether the minority shareholders can effectively establish breach of fiduciary duties. It would then be appropriate to examine the two requirements of 'fraud' and the 'control' element to bring the derivative action.

Purchase of the Piece of Land in South London

The piece of land that was purchased seems on the facts to have been an opportunity that A Ltd was pursuing. In *Regal (Hastings) Ltd* v *Gulliver* [1967] 2 AC 134, the House of Lords held that in equity, directors cannot put themselves in a position where as directors their duty to the company will conflict with their personal interests. The inflexible rule of equity would suggest that when the directors here were carrying out their duties in looking for investment opportunities, the property could be said to have been obtained only by reason of the fact that they were directors of A Ltd. There is, however, the point here in respect of the lack of funds on the part of A Ltd. In *Regal (Hastings)* the House of Lords was not prepared to accept the point that the company had no funds to accept the shares. The court in *Regal* was applying the principle in *Keech* v *Sandford* (1726) 25 ER 223 where the trustee was subject to a constructive trust of a lease even when it was impossible for the trust to obtain it.

The other point that has to be considered is the fact that John and Jane were also directors of B Ltd. This raises the issue of whether it could be asserted by A Ltd that the land was acquired by the directors as only being the directors of

A Ltd. It can be argued that in *Regal* the House of Lords posed the test as to whether the shares were obtained by the directors only by reason of being directors of Regal. In such circumstances A Ltd may not be able to get the directors to account. The point has not been clearly decided when directors act on behalf of both companies when obtaining a benefit.

Donations Amounting to £100,000 to Various Charities

This raises the issue of the duty imposed by the law on directors to act bona fide in the interests of the company. In *Re Smith & Fawcett Ltd* [1942] Ch 304, it was held that it was for the directors to decide what is in the interests of the company.

It is necessary for the directors to show that there is some reasonable grounds for believing that some act or acts are in the interests of the company. It is difficult to see how the donations of substantial sums when the company has been unable to pay dividends could be in the interests of the company. It has to be considered whether the phrase 'interests of the company' would cover the company as the commercial entity and this would be judged by the interests of present and future shareholders. It could also be argued here that the directors were also in breach of ther duties relating to the exercise of reasonable care and skill. In *Re D'Jan of London Ltd* [1993] BCC 646, it was said that the duty of care owed by a director at common law is accurately stated in section 214(4) of the Insolvency Act 1986. This would mean that the standard of care is one of a reasonably diligent person having both (a) the general knowledge, skill and experience that may reasonably be expected of a person carrying out the same functions as are carried out by that director in relation to the company and (b) the general knowledge, skill and experience that that director has.

Having considered the possibility of there being a breach of fiduciary duties, the minority shareholders have to now establish the elements of a derivative action. First we would have to consider 'fraud' and then 'control'.

Fraud

In *Menier* v *Hooper's Telegraph Works* (1874) LR 9 Ch App 350, it was held by the Court of Appeal that the fraud is to be tested by whether the majority shareholders have appropriated corporate assets. On our present facts the acquiring of the land could be argued, as in *Cook* v *Deeks* [1916] 1 AC 554, to be an opportunity belonging to A Ltd. But the difficulty here is that A Ltd like B Ltd did not have the necessary financial resources to deal with the purchase.

The breach here may not be a 'fraud'. On the position of the donations to the charities, this would certainly not constitute a fraud.

Control

Both John and Jane have control as they are majority shareholders. However, since there is no fraud here in relation to the breaches of fiduciary duty, John and Jane if they so choose can ratify.

In *Regal (Hastings) Ltd* v *Gulliver*, the House of Lords was prepared to accept that the members could have ratified the directors' breach of fiduciary duties. John and Jane, as held in *North-West Transportation Co. Ltd* v *Beatty* (1887) 12 App Cas 589, can vote in their own self-interest in view of there being no fraud.

Advice to the Liquidator of B Ltd

The liquidator would be concerned with section 214 of the Insolvency Act. By this provision, on the insolvent winding up of the company, the liquidator can seek a contribution by the directors of a company.

Here what has to be established is that John and Jane knew or ought to have concluded that there was no reasonable prospect that the company would avoid going into insolvent liquidation.

As to the purchase of the land in South London, as discussed earlier there is the difficulty of whether the opportunity to purchase the land arose by reason of John and Jane being directors of B Ltd alone.

If the liquidator of B Ltd wants to proceed against John and Jane, the proceedings would be on the basis of the breach of directors' fiduciary duties.

12 Investor Protection

INTRODUCTION

This is an area of company law that is tested in most exams on the basis of the Financial Services Act 1986. Company law exams do not require knowledge of the Stock Exchange listing regulation.

The Financial Services Act 1986 provides a statutory remedy for misrepresentations and omissions in listing and supplementary listing particulars. The Act actually provides two causes of action namely misrepresentation and omission, the other cause of action is for failure to issue relevant supplements.

There are also the common law remedies such as rescission of allotment and the liability for deceit that have to be considered.

It would be useful to read ch. 7 of *Mayson, French and Ryan on Company Law*.

QUESTION 1

The Financial Services Act 1986 has resolved the problem of providing an adequate remedy for someone suffering damage through an investment in a public company following inducement to make that investment by a material misrepresentation. Discuss.

Commentary

The question requires a consideration of the relevant provisions touching on the two causes of action based on misrepresentation and omissions and the other of not issuing relevant supplements.

It would also be necessary to consider the rationale for the framework of the 1986 Financial Services Act.

It would also be useful to consider the limitations of the common law remedies.

Suggested Answer

The government when proposing the Financial Services Act 1986 stated in the white paper that whilst market forces provide the best means of ensuring that the industry meets the needs of its customers, it is nevertheless necessary that as much information as possible is disclosed about the investments and services on offer to the customer. The government had also declared that the regulatory framework should aim for prevention, that is, to ensure that there is prevention as opposed to cure. The regulatory framework was to make fraud less likely to occur. The difficulty with the common law remedy was that any plaintiff, that is, the allottee, had to identify the statement that is dishonestly made. Following the House of Lords decision in *Derry* v *Peek* (1889) 14 App Cas 337, Parliament enacted the Directors Liability Act 1890 to deal with negligent statements in prospectuses. However, in respect of liability today under the Financial Services Act 1986 (FSA), section 47 covers cases where a person makes a statement, promise or forecast which he knows to be misleading, false or deceptive or dishonestly conceals material facts. At common law misrepresentation would not cover omissions. Section 47(1)(b) also goes on to state that there can be liability even if there is no dishonesty so long as there is a statement, promise or forecast which is misleading, false or deceptive. An important development brought in by section 47(2) of the FSA deals with the creation of a false or misleading impression as to the market in or price of any investment so as to induce another person to buy. The takeover by Guinness of

Distillers Co. plc could be treated as an example of an illegal share operation. Guinness here was issuing its own shares to shareholders of Distillers in return for their shares, it was essential to maintain the price of Guinness shares as the currency of purchase. The bidding company may encourage others to buy its shares by making loans to them or indemnifying them for any losses that might be incurred if they buy on a falling market.

The above provisions as to misrepresentation and omission by section 150(1) apply to listing particulars and section 166(1) extends liability for misrepresentation and omission in relation to prospectuses. The FSA also provides compensation to everyone who has acquired relevant securities (or any interest in such securities as provided by section 150(5) and section 166(5) and suffered a loss as a result of any untrue or misleading statement or the omission of anything required to be included by section 146(1) and section 163(1) respectively (this is the general duty of disclosure) or by section 147 and section 164 respectively (the duty to publish details of any significant new matter or change).

The FSA marks an improvement as to civil liability as the FSA refers to a person that has 'acquired' securities which includes both original allottees and persons who have purchased securities in the market. In *Peek* v *Gurney* (1873) LR 6 HL 377, it was held at Common Law that only the original allottees could sue in respect of a misrepresentation made in a prospectus inviting subscriptions for new shares. As for the measure of damages, in *Clark* v *Urquhart*[1930] AC 28, the measure of damages was held to be the same as in the tort of deceit. Section 150(1) and section 166(1) of the FSA use the term 'compensation' and it could be assumed here that the compensation is based on a tortious action. The other cause of action that has to be considered under the Act is the requirement of section 164 of the FSA, that a supplementary prospectus will be required in much the same way and on the same grounds as section 147 relating to supplementary listing particulars. This is to ensure notification to investors of any significant new matter that has arisen which would affect the reasonably informed investor in making an informed assessment of the issuers' assets, liabilities, financial position, results, prospects and the rights attached to the securities which are the subject of the prospectus.

The FSA provides for certain defences. By section 150(6) a person is not liable to pay compensation for failing to disclose information which he would not be required to disclose in listing particulars. By section 151(1) and section 167(1) a defendant would not be liable to pay compensation if he satisfies the court that he reasonably believed at the time the listing particulars were submitted to the Stock Exchange or the prospectus was delivered for registration as appropriate that the statement was true and not misleading or that the omission was proper. Also one additional fact out of four provided by the Act must be satisfied:

(a)   he continued to hold that belief until the securities were acquired, or

(b)   they were acquired before it was reasonably practicable to bring a correction to the attention of potential investors, or

(c)   before they were acquired he had taken all reasonable steps to bring a correction to the attention of potential investors, or

(d)   the securities were acquired after such a lapse of time that he ought reasonably to be excused and by section 151(1) he continued to hold the belief after the commencement of dealings in the securities following listing.

By section 151 and section 167 a defendant will not be liable to pay compensation for any loss caused by a statement purporting to be made by or on the authority of an expert which is stated to be included with the person's consent. The defendant must also satisfy the court that he reasonably believed in both the expert's competence and his consent to the inclusion of the statement in that form. The other defences set out in section 151 and section 167 of the FSA would cover matters such as the defendant having taken steps to correct defects and also where the defendant believed reasonably that the change or new matter in question was trivial and was not such as to call for supplementary listing particulars or a supplementary prospectus as appropriate.

In conclusion it can be seen that the FSA does show an improvement over the earlier common law and statutory remedies. The legislation does strike a balance between maintaining the principle of *caveat emptor* at the same time ensuring, as was stated in the report by Professor Gower, that regulation should be 'no greater than is necessary to protect reasonable people from being made fools of'. The FSA also, it can be stated, encourages high standards of conduct of investment business.

QUESTION 2

Do-it Right Ltd was a private company controlled by a family, and has now become a public limited company. Do-it Right plc now runs five shops all over London selling extremely simple to assemble furniture. The shops are under lease from various local authorities. The directors of Do-it Right Ltd, Sam and Jane Sattee, were advised by Bury Bank, a merchant bank, that fresh capital could be raised by issuing 5 million £1 shares and obtaining a listing on the Stock Exchange. The application to the Stock Exchange was successful. Listing particulars were published which stated that the turnover of Do-it Right Ltd was likely to increase by 50 per cent in 1999 and 2000 because of a big demand for such furniture and that Do-it Right had access to cheap raw materials. The statement of the increase in turnover was not stated in the accounts and was not taken into account in the profit forecast. The issue price was 150 pence per share and the flotation was successful with the price of shares rising steadily to 320 pence after the first month of trading. The listing particulars did not mention that three of the leases were due to expire before the listing and the local authorities are refusing to renew the leases. More recently it has emerged that because of changes in policies in countries where Do-it Right was receiving its raw materials it has become more costly to produce the furniture. Also a proposed EC Directive is going to require the company to change its method of production making it more costly.

The share price of Do-it Right has now fallen by 90 per cent.

Advise Tom who bought shares in Do-it Right on flotation by application from Bury bank, and Dick who purchased shares one month later when the shares were at their peak in the market.

Commentary

The question is a test of the basic structure of the provisions to be found in part IV of the Financial Services Act 1986 governing public issues of shares. There is also a need to consider section 130 of the 1985 Companies Act. Students should now consider the Public Offers of Securities Regulations 1995.

Suggested Answer

In advising both Tom and Dick it must be first pointed out that they would be concerned with the information in the listing particulars. The Financial Services Act 1986 (FSA) by section 150 imposes liability on person or persons responsible for any listing particulars in damages if a person acquiring securities in question have suffered loss in respect of the statements being untrue or misleading statements.

It must also be noted that it is immaterial that Dick has obtained the shares on the stock market. This is the case as, unlike the common law, Dick can also claim compensation so long as he is able to establish the misrepresentation or omission, even though he is not an original allottee. Section 150(5) of the FSA today provides that references in the section to the 'acquisition' covers any person who has contracted to acquire them or has an interest in them.

We can now consider the issue of misrepresentation or omissions. The position here is that when any plaintiff has established the presence of misrepresentation or omission and resulting loss, the burden then falls on the defendant to establish a defence if he is to avoid liability.

Misrepresentations and Omission

The listing particulars had stated that the company Do-it Right plc was likely to increase its turnover by 50 per cent in 1999 and 2000 because of the big demand for such furniture. This statement is not correct as the price of raw materials had increased and there was no basis for the statement. The omission to mention the non-renewal of the leases has affected the performance of the company.

Section 146 imposes a duty on those responsible for listing particulars to include information which investors and their professional advisers would reasonably expect to find for the purposes of making informed assessment of (a) the assets and liabilities, financial position, profits and losses, and prospects of the issue of the securities, and (b) the rights attaching to those securities.

It is important also to note that the information to be included would be that which is within the knowledge of any person responsible for the listing particulars or which it would be reasonable for him to obtain on making any enquiries.

Section 152 identifies the persons responsible for particulars as being the issuers of the securities and in this case by section 152(1)(b) it would be the directors of the company.

Possible Defences Open to Directors

By section 151 a person would not be liable to make compensation if it is possible to rely on exemptions to liability. This is covered by section 151. On our facts it is clear that the accounts do contain statements relating to the future profits. This could be an indication that the directors may have had a belief that the profits could increase. By section 151(1)(a) directors would not be liable only if they had a continued belief in the particulars. On the facts of the question there is no indication of the directors taking any steps to correct the statement in the listing particulars in relation to the price of raw materials.

The facts also do not indicate the use of an expert's opinion as part of the listing particulars. The issuers of the particulars could avoid liability if they relied on the opinion of an expert if they believed the expert was competent and had a belief that the statement was true at the time the securities were issued.

Claim for Compensation

By the scheme of the FSA the person or persons responsible for any listing particulars will be liable for compensation if there has been loss suffered as a result of the untrue of misleading statement in or omission from the listing particulars. Here in the case of both Tom and Dick they had clearly suffered loss as the value of the shares has dropped dramatically. It can also be stated here that the loss can be due to the misleading statement in the particulars or the omission from them under section 146.

A point that also has to be considered is the issuing of the shares at a premium. This is the case as the normal value of the shares is £1 and the shares were issued at 150 pence. The company, by section 130 of the Companies Act, has to treat the amount of the premium as part of its paid-up capital.

In dealing with the claim for damages, although at common law the measure of damages was tortious, the FSA only refers to 'compensation' and it could be argued that the measure of damages would also be on a tortious basis. Both Tom and Dick would be able to claim damages on the basis of the difference between what was paid at the time of issue or in the case of Dick at the time he purchased the shares on the stock market and the actual value of the shares. In Tom's case the premium would have to be taken into account.

There is no question of any contract of allotment being illegal as the law does permit shares being allotted at a premium.

In Tom's case since the shares were allotted by the company on flotation, he would have to repudiate the contract of allotment of shares to claim damages. This was decided in the House of Lords' decision of *Houldsworth* v *City of Glasgow Bank* (1880) 5 App Cas 317. However, under section 111A of the

Companies Act 1985 this rule would not apply. As it is possible to treat the term 'compensation' as being similar to the tortious measure of damages it could be argued the restriction imposed by the case of *Houldsworth* would still apply.

A Claim in Negligence

Tom, being the original allottee, could also bring a claim in negligence. The claim can be based on negligent misstatement as the directors should have been aware of the effect of the non-renewal of the leases on the business and also the increase in the cost of raw materials should also have been taken into account when dealing with the statement in the prospectus. However, as held in *Al-Nakib Investments (Jersey) Ltd* v *Longcroft* [1990] 1 WLR 1390, the duty of care would not be owed by the company to other purchasers such as Dick and here in the market. The court proceeded on the basis that the preparation of the prospectus was for the purpose of inviting the original allottees, but even if relied upon by Dick, the use of the prospectus would be for a purpose other than that for which it was prepared.

13   Insider Dealings

INTRODUCTION

This is quite a controversial area of company law with very deeply diverging views among academics. There is a good selection of background materials in ch. 19 of *Cases and Materials on Company Law* by Andrew Hicks and S.H. Goo. There is now part V of the Criminal Justice Act 1993 which is the remodelled legislation. It has repealed the Company Securities (Insider Dealing) Act 1985. The area of insider trading can also be seen as part of investor protection in terms of maintaining confidence in the stock market generally. You should also here observe that the Treaty obligations of the United Kingdom under the Treaty of Rome have resulted in the influence of the Council Directive of 13 November 1989 on co-ordinating regulations on insider dealing.

QUESTION 1

Insider dealing has been a criminal offence since 1980 in English law. Examine the justification for making it a criminal offence and whether English law has on the whole provided an effective remedy.

Commentary

A complex question that requires some knowledge of the jurisprudence in this area. Reference has aleady been made to the material set out in the case book by Hicks and Goo. There is also the analysis by T. Michael Ashe (1990) 11 Co. Law 127.

Suggested Answer

To begin with it is necessary to consider the rationale for the law making insider trading an offence. The widely accepted view is that by ensuring such a law it would provide investor confidence in the market. It is thus argued that for markets to be successful they depend on the flow and the availability of information on the liquidity of dealings.

The moment information is not available equally to all potential investors then the market will be seen as unfair and this will be damaging to investor confidence. The view that is held by some is that there are two main kinds of information in valuing shares in a company. They are first information about the economy and world trade which is available to all and secondly information about how the company itself is handling its affairs. Insider dealing takes place when information is first known to people who are 'insiders'. That is close to the company itself, and when the rest of the market is denied the information, this is seen as an abuse of the directors' position also. This is the case as the directors' use the information to their advantage at the expense of the shareholders who appointed them. There is, however, the view expressed by Professor Manne, a lawyer and economist, who stated that the insider dealing in shares will in effect affect the price in the market to the true worth of the shares indirectly as the information about those shares is released to the market by the insider dealing in it. Professor Manne's definition of insider dealing requires one to consider seriously the issue of unfairness. The argument that is often put forward is that at least in anonymous market transactions the person who happens to deal with the insider is a willing purchaser or seller in the market-place at that point in time. If there is no misleading by the insider, then it can be seriously questioned where the unfairness is.

In the United States the view that unfairness has been established when the insider uses privileged information can be compared to the young law student's response of 'I don't care, its just not right'.

This view follows from Professor Manne's argument that there is no unfairness from taking advantage of privileged information if there is no demonstrable harm. However, when the Criminal Justice Bill introduced the present insider dealing provisions Earl Ferrers observed that 'in order to operate successfully, those markets require investors to have confidence in their fairness. Insider dealing destroys that confidence'.

More recently studies have shown that insider dealing inflates the cost of raising funds in the stock market since investors will pay less for shares floated in markets which they think are rigged.

English law finally in the 1980 Companies Act made insider dealing a criminal offence on the basis that it is a wrong to the market. The provisions were re-enacted with minor amendments in the Company Securities (Insider Dealing) Act 1985. The recent Criminal Justice Act 1993, whilst retaining some of the key concepts, reflects a different philosophy from earlier enactments. Whilst the aim was to maintain confidence in the market, the 1993 Act does not require the necessary information to be confidential. Also it is not necessary for the insider to be connected with either the source of the relevant information or the issue of the securities in question. The developments in respect of insider dealing lead to an emphasis on the disclosure. If price sensitive information which is withheld from the market is kept to a minimum, there will be less opportunity for those desirous of exploiting it. Today by section 324 of the Companies Act 1985, a director is under an obligation to notify the company in writing of his shares of the company and debentures.

Over the years there have been difficulties in being able to bring successful prosecutions. The reasons for this can be stated to be not only the lack of manpower and resources as far as the Department of Trade and Industry is concerned but there is also the issue of whether there should be a separate agency. An example of a specialised agency is Singapore's Commercial Affairs Department. The department was set up in 1985. It has a professional staff of about 50. Most are trained investigators, and some are police officers on secondment to the department. In addition there are in-house State prosecutors. Each time a case comes in one of the lawyers is assigned. Accordingly in each investigation a lawyer is involved and ultimately when the matter goes to court the lawyer can be part of the prosecution team. Insider trading is an offence that requires a great deal of investigative work. Failure to ascertain sufficient facts or poor court work can lead to a collapse of the prosecution. In the United Kingdom at the moment the Secretary of State has power to appoint inspectors if it appears that there are circumstances suggesting that there may have been a breach of part of the Criminal Justice Act 1993. This approach would certainly not be that effective in respect of enforcement even if the legislative framework is adequate.

The 1993 Criminal Justice Act now is more focused on the control of securities market than the abuse of confidential information. However, all this is not going to make any difference if the enforcement aspect has not been dealt with. There is now a trend seen in South Africa and more recently in Singapore where legislation now enables the prosecution to prove a case of insider dealing on a 'balance of probabilities' as opposed to 'beyond a reasonable doubt'.

Also legislation in South Africa and Singapore now enables the authorities to bring civil actions to recover damages.

In South Africa since May 1999 when the changes to the law were brought in a sum of 2.2 million rand was recovered in six insider dealing cases over an eight-month period. This is in great contrast to the position prior to the changes in the law when not even a single case was prosecuted in 112 years.

Another suggestion has been to introduce a simple penalty system. This would mean that the prosecution serves a statement of facts on the insider and if the facts are not accepted then it can be dealt with by the appropriate civil tribunal. The tribunal can then determine a penalty on the basis of a multiple of the gain made or loss avoided as well as confiscate the gain.

It is possible that the penalty system together with more resources into investigation would be more helpful in deterring insider dealing.

QUESTION 2

Wellybob plc is a listed company that has diverse business activities. Mark is an employee working in the accounts department of the company. One afternoon during lunch Mark had heard from a director that the company just a few hours ago had heard from Malaysia that the Malaysian government had approved of an important joint venture. The director had stated that the information had come from the managing director, Lord Wellybob himself.

That evening on his way home Mark had met June, his girlfriend, and had told her that as soon as the Malaysian joint venture was announced the shares of Wellybob plc would pick up in price as Wellybob plc was the only British company that had received the approval for the venture. He wanted June to obtain further shares and sell them when the shares reached their peak.

June made a profit by selling the Wellybob plc shares a few days later.

It has also transpired that Pillai, a director of Wellybob plc, had purchased the shares in the company from Lawrence, a shareholder, without informing him of the venture in Malaysia. Pillai had then made a profit from the sale of the shares. Advise Mark, June and Pillai of any liability under part V of the Criminal Justice Act 1993. Also Lawrence now wants to be advised on any rights against Pillai.

Commentary

The question requires the consideration of the basic elements involved in establishing insider dealing under part V of the Criminal Justice Act 1993.

There is also an aspect of the director's position in relation to a shareholder in relation to price sensitive information.

Suggested Answer

It would be necessary in order to consider the liability of Mark to consider first his position in relation to the information he possesses. By section 56 of the 1993 Act the information here is specific information which can significantly affect the price of securities. Section 60(4) provides that information must be treated as relating to a company where it can affect the company's business prospects.

Also at the time Mark heard of the Malaysian venture the information was not derived from any source that was public and also it was not in any way public within the meaning of section 58(2). The market here is clearly a regulated market as the shares are listed on the Stock Exchange.

When considering the offence of insider dealing what is important is that the information must be information that a party possesses as an insider. The 1993 Act restricts what may be done by an individual who has information as an insider. By section 57(1) of the Act an individual will have information as an insider if he or she knows that it is inside information and if, as in the facts of this question, the source of the information is a director. Section 57(2)(b) covers persons who are sometimes referred to as 'tippees'.

Mark has committed an offence under section 52(2)(a) by encouraging another person to deal in shares whose price would be affected by his inside information, knowing or having reasonable cause to believe that the dealing being encouraged would take place. Mark can be prosecuted only with the consent of the Secretary of State or the Director of Public Prosecutions. On indictment the penalty can be imprisonment for up to seven years and/or a fine for which there is no limit.

Liability of June

June profited from information that is insider information. She does also possess that information as an insider.

This is the case as by section 57(1) she knows that the information is inside information and also by section 57(2) the information is from an inside source as John is an employee of the company. Finally June has committed an offence as she has by section 55(1) dealt in the securities by disposing of the securities.

Liability of Pillai

In considering Pillai's liability it would not only be necessary to consider liability in relation to insider dealing, but also the question of whether Lawrence would have any claim against him. Pillai has information as an insider because he has it through being a director of the company, and when he acquires the shares from Lawrence, there is a 'dealing' in the securities within the meaning of section 55(1) of the Act.

Having established the basis of the liability under part V of the Criminal Justice Act 1993, the next point that has to be considered is whether there can be any civil liability concerning Lawrence.

Question of Civil Liability Concerning Lawrence

English law generally takes the position that directors owe fiduciary duties to the company and not to individual shareholders. In the leading case of *Percival v Wright* [1902] 2 Ch 421, it was held by Swinfen Eady J that directors had no duty when negotiating a sale of shares to disclose information that could have an effect on the valuaton of the shares. Here it is quite clear that Lawrence's shares would be worth more at the time of Pillai's purchase and Lawrence would not have parted with the shares at a particular price if he had known about the information.

In recent years *Percival* v *Wright* has not been followed particularly by the Commonwealth authorities. In *Coleman* v *Myers* [1977] 2 NZLR 225 the New Zealand Court of Appeal stated that they were not following *Percival* v *Wright*. The New Zealand Court of Appeal expressed the view that a director may have to assume responsibility to a shareholder depending on the surrounding circumstances and the nature of the responsibility which in a real and practical sense the director has assumed towards the shareholder.

In *Coleman* v *Myers* the fiduciary duty was said to arise from the family character of the company and the high degree of insider knowledge possessed by the directors. It may be argued here on our facts that Pillai owed a fiduciary duty in view of the price-sensitive nature of the information. Also it must be noted here that any transaction that is in contravention of part V of the Act must stand and it is not void or voidable. This is provided by section 63(2).

The other point to note here is that since Pillai is a fiduciary, any profits he makes by occupying that position would belong to the person to whom the duty is owed. Thus it has been held in the United States of America in *Diamond* v *Oreamuno* (1969) 248 NE 2d 910, that if a director of a company buys or sells shares as a result of information about the company obtained by virtue of the directorship then the profit belongs to the company. The only way the director can retain a benefit is if the company expressly agrees to this.

14   Company Insolvency

INTRODUCTION

The area of insolvency has been becoming more and more important in recent years. Many company law cases today focus upon this area.

You are advised here to be familiar with the scheme of the 1986 Insolvency Act where there is now the introduction of the administrator and the administrative receiver. Further there is also a need to be familiar with the procedures of the Act relating to the setting aside of particular transactions or the setting aside of charges. It would also be useful here to relate the material in this section with what is covered in the chapter on loan capital. This area, whilst often tested on its own, can also form part of a question because aspects of the Insolvency Act now influence so many areas of company law that it can also turn up in other areas.

You would find it useful here to read ch. 20 of *Mayson, French and Ryan on Company Law*, entitled Company Insolvency and Liquidation.

Cases and Materials on Company Law by Andrew Hicks and S.H. Goo at ch. 20 provides useful background into the Cork Committee Report and the purposes of corporate insolvency law. This chapter is entitled Corporate Insolvency.

QUESTION 1

Assess the effectiveness of the Insolvency Act 1986 in achieving the aims of protecting the interests of creditors and ensuring that the company is able to work out any financial difficulties so as to be able to survive.

Commentary

The question requires a sound knowledge of the purposes of insolvency law and the framework of the Insolvency Act 1986.

Suggested Answer

The Insolvency Act 1986 highlights the need for corporate insolvency law to strike a balance between debtor and creditor and at the same time gives the chance for companies to rescue parts of a business or the whole of the business. If we begin by considering the position with regard to the administrative receiver we would see how the Act deals with the objections identified above. The appointment of the administrative receiver would only take place in the case of a company which is insolvent as opposed to one that is solvent. The administrative receiver is appointed by a creditor or creditors that have a floating charge over all or a substantial part of the company's assets. The administrative receiver is an agent of the company unless and until it goes into liquidation. The directors of the company would no longer have any authority to deal with the charged property, but the directors continue in office and are still liable to submit returns and documents to the registrar. From *Smiths Ltd* v *Middleton* [1979] 3 All ER 842, it is evident that the administrative receiver of a company must provide directors with whatever information they require to carry out their residual duties. Also information about assets should be given to directors if they want to re-arrange finance.

The 1986 Act also requires the administrative receiver to submit a report to creditors within three months of the appointment pursuant to section 48. The report should also include any statement of affairs submitted to the receiver by the directors and the receiver's comments (if any). The administrative receiver would then also be required to summon a meeting of the unsecured creditors, unless the court orders otherwise.

The Insolvency Act also introduced the concept of the administrator. The government agreed with the Cork Committee that an alternative insolvency mechanism to be known as the administrator procedure should be established.

The idea here is that the appointment of the administrator will provide a valuable addition to existing insolvency procedures. The procedure will provide a more effective method of achieving rehabilitation or reorganisation than receivership or where there are no floating charges under which a receiver could be appointed.

It was also accepted by the government that since the administrator would manage the company to an extent that was similar to receivers who were also managers whenever there is an application for an administrator, the floating charge holder, who can appoint an administrative receiver, should be able to appoint an administrative receiver and prevent an administrator being appointed.

The provisions concerning this in sections 8, 9 and 11 of the Act touch on this important innovation. Section 8 of the Act sets out the various grounds on which a petition can be presented to obtain an administration order. In *Re Harris Simons Construction Ltd* [1989] 1 WLR 368, the court held that when considering under section 8(1)(b) whether survival is 'likely' the approach is to consider if there is some real prospect of the administration order enabling the whole or part of the company's undertaking surviving or the administration order ensuring a more advantageous realisation of the assets than on a winding up.

In *Re Harris Simons Construction* the court concluded that the test of whether an administrative order should be made is based on a possibility of the aims being achieved. The court also considered the Cork Committee proposals on this where on recommending administration the Committee had noted that it should be used only where there is a sufficient substance to justify the expense of an administration and where there is a real prospect of returning to profitability or selling as a going conern. The administration order would also bring in a moratorium on enforcement of debts and proceedings cannot also be commenced against the company while the order is in force.

In *Re Harris Simons* the court saw the importance of the administration order in view of how sometimes the company would require the breathing space so as to raise further finance or for a more advantageous realisation of the company's assets. The court thus was prepared to resort to a very much lower test of the possibility of achieving the aims of the administration order as opposed to the probability of achieving the aims. In *Re Atlantic Computer Systems plc* [1992] Ch 505, the Court of Appeal had to consider the administrator's obligations on long-term leases. The Court of Appeal concluded that whilst the language of the 1986 Act may be brief, what is clear is that the moratorium on enforcement of security and debts is such as to encourage as much as possible the rescue while not expropriating property of third parties.

Turning now to the introduction of fraudulent and wrongful trading, the concept of fraudulent trading, which was introduced in 1929, was to ensure that directors do not trade to defraud creditors. The difficulty with this is proving the intention to defraud creditors. The Insolvency Act 1986 by section 213 retains the concept of fraudulent trading. The heavy burden on the liquidator to prove dishonesty led the Cork Committee to introduce the new concept of wrongful trading. Section 214 permits the liquidator to obtain a court order to require a director or shadow director to contribute to the assets of the company to compensate creditors generally for the loss caused by their wrongful trading.

Section 214(2)(b) refers to the knowledge on the part of a director in terms of when he knew or ought to have known that the company could not avoid going into insolvent liquidation. By section 214(3) the director has an objective duty not to increase creditors' losses. The Cork Committee in introducing section 214 wanted to strike a balance in respect of encouraging the inception and growth of businessess and preventing downright irresponsibility. The decision of *Re Produce Marketing Consortium Ltd (No. 2)* [1989] BCLC 520, shows that whilst judges are prepared to consider the particular company and its business, they insist that a director should be aware of accounting facts or figures if, with reasonable diligence and an appropriate level of skill, he ought to have ascertained them.

One can state here that a higher objective standard as opposed to a lower subjective standard has been imposed by section 214(4) of the Insolvency Act 1986 towards creditors.

In conclusion, it could be said that the Insolvency Act has been a successful framework in achieving the two objects of enabling companies to deal more effectively with difficulties encountered by a business and also ensuring that abuses in the insolvency law prior to 1986 have been reduced or completely removed.

QUESTION 2

John is the majority shareholder and the managing director of 'John of Arabia' Ltd (the company), specialising in the supply of Arabian horses and other exotic animals to fairs and zoos. John had loaned the company £50,000 in 1999 when the company was doing relatively well. However, by 2000 things were not going so well, as animal rights activist have increased campaigning and the importation of the animals has dropped. John then caused the company to grant him a charge expressed as a fixed charge over its business premises and book debts. The company's bank, Borrings Bank, after pressing the company to provide security in relation to its overdraft facilities, now has been able to get the company to grant a floating charge over all its assets. The charge was granted in February 2000. The company's accountant has been presenting the financial position to John regularly and explaining that unless he does something 'drastic' the company would go into insolvent liquidation. John ignored all this and now a creditor has presented a winding-up petition on the grounds that the company is insolvent. Advise John who is now concerned about his liability if any and the position concerning the various charges. Assume that all the charges were duly registered.

Commentary

The question touches on the setting aside of charges, that is, to consider if there is a preference. Also one has to consider the wrongful trading provision of section 214 of the Insolvency Act. The question also shows how questions dealing with the area of fixed and floating charges can involve issues of the Insolvency Act.

Suggested Answer

Nature of the Charges on Book Debts

The charge on the book debts does cause a difficulty as it is not how the charge is described in the debentures that identifies its status rather the characteristics of the charge. In *Re New Bullas Trading Ltd* [1994] 1 BCLC 485 the court held that a charge on book debts may be validly created as a fixed charge while the debts remain uncollected, only if the company and the creditor agree that there are to be restrictions on the dealings with the book debts. In the *New Bullas* case, the debenture required the money raised from the book debts to be paid into a specific bank account.

On our facts there are no details of how the book debts are to be dealt with when the charge has been created. In these circumstances following the approach in *Siebe Gorman & Co. Ltd* v *Barclays Bank Ltd* [1979] 2 Lloyd's Rep 142, a charge would be determined to be a floating charge in the case of book debts if it allows the company the freedom to deal with the money after the company's debtors have paid the sums.

Preference under Section 239 of the Insolvency Act 1986

By this section if within the 'relevant time', the company does anything or suffers anything to be done that has the effect of putting a creditor in a position which, in the event of the company going into insolvent liquidation, will be better than if the thing had not been done then the court may make an order restoring the position to what it would have been if the preference had not been given.

The relevant time if the creditor is a 'connected' person is two years ending with the onset of insolvency (sections 240(1)(a) and 249).

The onset of insolvency here is, by section 240(3), to be when the winding-up petition was filed. In the circumstances the charge created in favour of John is within the two-year period.

Turning now to the requirements of the preference. In *Re MC Bacon Ltd* [1990] BCLC 372, it was held that under section 239 there is no longer a need to show a dominant intention to prefer as was required under section 44 of the Bankruptcy Act 1914. Under section 239 all that is required is to show that at the time the charge was created the decision was influenced by a desire to prefer. The other aspect identified in the decision is that under section 239 there is no longer a need to show an intention to prefer as in section 44 of the Bankruptcy Act as section 239 refers to the desire. Desire is considered to be subjective. On our facts it is clear that when the company granted the charge to John the desire was to improve his position as a creditor in the event of insolvent liquidation. This is the case as he knew that the business was not doing well. There also does not seem to be any possibility of arguing that John had a belief that the company could be pulled around.

In conclusion here the liquidator can obtain an order from the court to deal with the assets on the basis that the company did not create a charge on the assets.

Validity of the Charge in Favour of the Borrings Bank

The issue here is whether the charge created in favour of the bank can be set aside. A liquidator would be concerned with either a preference under section 239 of the Insolvency Act 1986, or alternatively section 245 which enables the liquidator to set aside a floating charge.

The question of a preference here would not arise as it cannot be said on the facts that the desire on the part of the company is to effect a preference. The facts indicate clearly that the company was subject to pressure by the bank. The function of section 245 of the Insolvency Act has now to be considered.

On the winding up of a company, section 245 of the Act permits it to avoid a floating charge except to the extent of the value of so much of the consideration for the creation of the charge which consists of money paid or goods or services supplied to the company at the same time as or after the creation of the charge. The other situation covered by section 245 is only to enable the charge to be enforced to the value of so much of the consideration as consists of the discharge or reduction at the same time as or after the creation of the charge of any debt of the company. The Cork Committee concluded that there may be advantages in permitting a creditor to take a charge and allow the company to continue in business rather than to press immediately for payment. This is in line with permitting companies in difficulties to work out the difficulties.

On our facts since the charge is to secure the overdraft facilities all withdrawals of money by the company or the honouring of cheques drawn by the bank would be consideration for the charge. In the circumstances the liquidator would find it difficult to disregard the floating charge.

John Continuing to Trade when Knowing of the Company's Difficulties

John would have to be advised here that the liquidator would be concerned with section 214 of the Insolvency Act 1986 which deals with wrongful trading and section 213 which deals with fraudulent trading.

In *Re Produce Marketing Consortium Ltd (No. 2)* [1989] BCLC 520, the court held that section 214 was different from fraudulent trading. What is required under section 214 is to consider whether a director knew or ought to have concluded that there was no reasonable prospect of the company avoiding going into insolvent liquidation. There is no need to establish any fraudulent intent. In *Re Produce Marketing Consortium* the court confirmed that directors should be receiving financial information, and a director cannot plead ignorance of accounting facts and figures. In this question there is knowledge of the figures by John who has carried on trading with adequate opportunity to know that something has to be done.

In *Re Produce Marketing* the court treated section 214 as being primarily compensatory rather than penal. Therefore if the court decides that John is going to be liable to contribute towards the company's assets, the sum can be quite substantial whether or not there is fraudulent intent. On the question of fraudulent trading there is a need to consider *R v Grantham* [1984] QB 675. The court there held that it is necessary to show that the accused knew at the time of incurring the debts that there was no reasonable prospect that the creditors would be paid when they expect to be paid. On our facts even after the accountant had presented the accounts and had stated clearly that something drastic had to be done, John nevertheless carried on trading. There is nothing on the facts to show any indication that John honestly believed in the company recovering.

QUESTION 3

(a)   Consider if there are any fiduciary duties owed by directors to creditors of an insolvent company.

(b)   B Ltd is a company which operates a small bookshop. In the last year or so the only directors and shareholders were Mary and Mark. Mary was paid her directors' remuneration as permitted by the articles even though because of illness she did not work in the bookshop. Mark was not well educated, although he had been running the bookshop for some 10 years. The company now has got liabilities exceeding its assets and a winding-up order has been made. Advise the liquidator as to whether there is any way that Mary and/or Mark can be made to contribute towards the company's assets.

Commentary

Part (a) requires a discussion of how the case law has approached defining the scope of director's duties. Also there has to be consideration of how section 214(4) has provided an objective test of fiduciary duties.

With regard to (b) the advice is going to be on the basis of the liquidator only being concerned with the statutory provisions in the Insolvency Act 1986 dealing with misfeasance and fraudulent trading. Also the common law has to be considered particularly on the issue of unlawful return of capital to shareholders and how liquidators can rely on these principles.

Suggested Answer

(a)   At common law directors owe fiduciary duties to the company and this has been defined in *Re Smith & Fawcett Ltd* [1942] Ch 304 as being a duty to act bona fide in what they consider is in the interests of the company. The difficulty with the term 'interests of the company' is that it does not become clear what the different interests are.

In *Hutton* v *West Cork Railway Co.* (1883) 23 ChD 654, the directors were said to act in the interests of the company if they consider the interests of the company as a corporate entity.

However, in recent years statute since the 1980 Companies Act enables directors to take into account the interests of employees when dealing with the interests of the members.

As far as Commonwealth authorities are concerned, in *Teck Corporation Ltd* v *Millar* (1972) 33 DLR (3d) 288, Berger J suggested that a company's interests should be defined more widely to include the interests of the company's employees and 'the community'.

In New Zealand and Australia the courts were aware of the effect of actions of directors on the company's assets and how this would affect creditors. Thus in *Kinsela* v *Russell Kinsela Pty Ltd* (1986) 4 NSWLR 722, Street CJ said that if a company is solvent the property interests of the shareholders entitle them as a general body to be regarded as the company when questions of the duty of directors arise. On the other hand if a company is insolvent the interests of the creditors would intrude and that prospectively creditors are entitled through the mechanism of liquidation to displace the power of the shareholders and directors to deal with the company's assets. The principle stated in the *Kinsela* case was accepted as part of English law by the Court of Appeal in *West Mercia Safetywear Ltd* v *Dodd* [1988] BCLC 250. In that case Mr Dodd was a director of A.J. Dodd & Co. Ltd and of its wholly owned subsidiary, West Mercia Safetywear Ltd. Mr Dodd had guaranteed the overdraft of the parent company. Even though advised by an accountant to put the parent and subsidiary into creditors' voluntary liquidation, he was not prepared to do so. When a debtor of West Mercia had paid a sum of money Mr Dodd transferred that money from West Mercia's account to the parent company so that he could reduce his liability on the guarantee.

The liquidator brought misfeasance proceedings against Dodd and he was made personally liable.

In conclusion one might state that since the Insolvency Act of 1986 the liquidator would be able to rely on the wrongful trading provision and the standard by section 214(4) of the 1986 Act imposes an objective test which does to a certain extent take into account subjective considerations such as the general knowledge, skill and experience of the particular director.

(b) Advice to the liquidator.

Mary's Remuneration

In *Re Halt Garage* (1964) Ltd [1982] 2 All ER 1016, the court held that a liquidator of a company was entitled to treat payments to shareholders who were directors as being an unlawful return of capital. On our facts it would appear that Mary is carrying out very little in terms of providing her services to the company.

Re Halt Garage would therefore suggest that even if payments can be treated as remuneration within the meaning of the articles, it is the amounts that the liquidator would be concerned with. If the company at the material time was solvent then shareholders could approve whatever payments that they consider suitable so long as it is within the company's profits.

The question here of what amounts to and would constitute remuneration is quite uncertain. However, what emerges from the *Re Halt Garage* decision is that if payments are treated as disguised capital being returned to a shareholder then it would be *ultra vires* in the sense that the act is illegal.

The conclusion that seems to follow from *Re Halt Garage* is that a liquidator can decide with objective scrutiny that a payment is excessive even if the directors such as on our facts may have acted honestly and have exercised powers that are within the capacity of the company.

Following the case of *Aveling Barford Ltd* v *Perion Ltd* (1989) 5 BCC 677, it has also to be noted that once an act is treated as being a disguised return of capital then even if all shareholders agree to the payment the payment would be illegal. Also in the *Aveling Barford* case the company was for all purposes solvent and was a going concern. However, if the transaction is treated as an illegal payment of capital to shareholders it cannot be ratified.

The development in *Re Halt Garage* and *Aveling Barford* does strengthen the position of insolvency practitioners. The advantage which this approach has is that there is no need to consider any 'relevant time' for the purposes of dealing with transactions at undervalue.

Liability of Mark and Mary for Fraudulent Trading or Wrongful Trading

Finding that directors had carried on with the business despite its difficulties the liquidator would want to consider first of all the possibility of establishing fraudulent trading. Following the decision in *R v Grantham* [1984] QB 675, the liquidator can establish an intention to defraud creditors if there is an intention to dishonestly prejudice the creditors in receiving payment of their debts. Mark, the facts indicate, is someone who is not very educated and if he honestly felt that the company would be able to recover then the element of dishonesty would not be established. Turning now to wrongful trading within the meaning of section 214 of the Insolvency Act 1986. Following *Re Produce Marketing Consortium Ltd (No. 2)* [1989] BCLC 520, it is important to start by noting that the standard in section 214(2) would ensure that anyone who is a director would be judged objectively in terms of considering what decisions the directors should have arrived at, on the basis that the company cannot reasonably avoid going into insolvent liquidation. As for section 214(4), considering the facts which a director of a company ought to know or ascertain and the conclusions which he ought to reach, the court in *Re Produce Marketing* confirmed that it can take into account not only documents that the directors had knowledge of but also other matters they ought to have known about.

Mark, being in the business for about 10 years, should be aware of the drop in any turnover and should be aware of the losses being incurred. It is also not clear whether the level of remuneration drawn was the same and there does not seem to have been any attempt to alter the business.

The liquidator could get Mark to contribute towards the company's assets and the money would be received for the benefit of all the creditors including persons who became creditors after Mark ought to have known of the company's inability to avoid going into insolvent liquidation.

QUESTION 4

Daniel is the sole director and shareholder (apart from one share held by Fifi, his wife) of Alpha Ltd, a company dealing with the supply of computer software. Some of the computer programs were produced by Daniel and supplied to his company pursuant to a separate agreement. The company had entered into various contracts with John Desk Top and Diana Digital which concern contracts to produce computer programs for the company.

From early 2000 the company has been hit by difficulties particularly because of the recession. The overdraft with the Bank of Cash and Credit reached some £300,000 by the end of 1999. The bank demanded security and in February 2000 Daniel granted a floating charge over all the undertakings to the bank as well as a fixed charge over all its book debts. Despite attempts to deal with the financial difficulties in the period from February to May 2000, the company suffered further losses. But prospects are good with the upturn in the economy in the future.

In May of 2000 the Bank of Cash and Credit discovered the following matters:

(a)   That the company had taken delivery of some computers, computer monitor screens and other computer accessories that have been supplied under contracts with retention of title provisions.

(b)   That Daniel had caused the company to repay to him a loan that he had made to the company in 1999 and also to pay him for work that he had done for the company in late 1999. All this came to £50,000.

(c)   That the company owed Diana Digital and John Desktop a sum of about £10,000.

(d)   That the commissioners of Customs and Excise were pressing for VAT payment arrears of some £15,000.

A petition has now been presented for the appointment of an administrator to the company.

The company's total assets are probably not worth more than £100,000. Advise the bank which is considering the appointment of an administrative receiver.

Commentary

The question requires a consideration of the nature of the bank's charge on the company's assets and the relative advantages and disadvantages of allowing the company to appoint an administrator, if this is possible, as opposed to the bank appointing an administrative receiver. The question covers an important area of the present insolvency law and that is the regime of administrative receivership.

Suggested Answer

It would be necessary first in advising the bank to consider the nature of the charges. The main concern of the bank would be with what is expressed to be a fixed charge over the company's book debts. It is important to consider if the charge restricts dealings with the proceeds of debts once the company has collected the money from its debtors.

Did the bank when creating the fixed charge on book debts require the proceeds to be paid into the company's account with the bank? In *Siebe Gorman & Co. Ltd* v *Barclays Bank Ltd* [1979] 2 Lloyd's Rep 142, the court had to decide whether a charge on book debts was a fixed or a floating charge. Slade J took the three characteristics of a floating charge listed by Romer LJ in *Re Yorkshire Woolcombers Association Ltd* [1903] 2 Ch 284, that (a) it is a charge on a class of assets present and future, (b) the class is one which, in the ordinary course of business of the company, would be changing from time to time, (c) the charge contemplates that, until some future step is taken by the chargee, the company may carry on its business in the ordinary way as far as concerns that particular class of assets. A charge on book debts has the first two characteristics: it is a charge on a class of present and future assets which would be continually changing as, when payment has been made to the company of existing debts, other debts would arise as further invoices are rendered. However, the terms of the charge contract in the *Siebe Gorman* case required all the proceeds of the book debts to be paid into the company's bank account and forbade the company from charging or assigning the debts without the bank's consent. Slade J concluded that this meant the third characteristic was not present and that the charge was a fixed charge, even though the company had breached the contract by assigning the debts.

The next issue that has to be considered is the position of the fixed charge on the book debts in the event of the charge being crystallised. By section 40 of the Insolvency Act 1986 the preferential debts such as the claim by the Commissioners of Customs and Excise would only have priority if the charge was created as a floating charge. As it seems that the charge as created was a floating charge, any receiver appointed cannot realise the assets without paying the preferential debt owed to the Commissioners of Customs and Excise.

Appointment of an Administrative Receiver

In the 1986 Insolvency Act, section 29(2) defines an 'administrative receiver' as a receiver or manager of the whole (or substantially the whole) of a company's property who is appointed by the holder or holders of any debenture which when created was a floating charge. As the bank is in a position to appoint an administrative receiver it is entitled by section 9(2) of the Insolvency Act to receive notice of a petition for an administrator. By section 9(3) an appointment by the bank of an administrative receiver would result in the court dismissing an application for an administrator. The appointment of the administrative receiver from the bank's point of view would give it an opportunity to take over the management of the company if it is concerned about the quality of the management of the administrator the court may appoint.

One point that the bank has to observe here with section 9 of the Insolvency Act is that if the charge can be set aside pursuant to section 245 or section 243 of the Insolvency Act, then the administrator would be appointed if the company is able to satisfy the requirements of section 8 of the Insolvency Act 1986.

On our facts when the company granted the charge it was for future facilities and here the bank would have furnished consideration. This would mean that the floating charge granted in favour of the bank would not be set aside under section 245 of the Act. Also since there is the pressure being placed by the bank it could be said that the intention of the company is not to provide a preference under section 243 of the Act.

The next issue that the bank is going to be concerned with is the relative benefits of appointing an administrative receiver as opposed to the appointment of an administrator. On our facts the bank should be advised that if it appoints an administrative receiver it will cause the crystallisation of the floating charge and at the same time, besides recovering what is due, can ensure that the business of the company is organised sufficiently well to deal with an anticipated increase in business.

However, there would appear to be a preference being made by the company under section 239 of the Insolvency Act 1986, in favour of Daniel. These matters can be dealt with by the administrator. The bank here should also be concerned with the possibility of the creditors, Diana Digital and John Desktop, presenting winding-up petitions and in such a circumstance the company's assets would have to be distributed on a break-up basis and not as a going concern.

The bank should be advised here that in the event of an administrator being appointed, by section 15 of the Insolvency Act 1986 the administrator can dispose of property subject to floating charges free of the charge with the charge holder's interest being in the proceeds.

On the whole it would be better for the bank to appoint an administrative receiver to ensure that the business is managed well. Although the preferential debts would have to be paid out of the assets subject to the floating charge, it is better for the bank to intervene at this stage, than to allow the company to seek an administration order which would then prevent the bank enforcing its security because of the moratorium that is introduced by section 11 of the Insolvency Act.

QUESTION 5

[Counsel for the Bank] suggested '. . . It would be technical for us to distinguish between parent and subsidiary company in this context; economically . . . they are one. But we are concerned not with economics but with law. The distinction between the two is, in law, fundamental and cannot be bridged'. Per Robert Goff LJ in *Bank of Tokyo Ltd* v *Karoon* [1987] AC 45. Discuss.

Commentary

The passage of Robert Goff LJ highlights one of the controversies that has been raging in English company law for some time. The thrust of the question requires consideration of what is sometimes referred to as the enterprise entity theory in English law.

Suggested Answer

The passage by Robert Goff LJ in the *Bank of Tokyo Ltd* case refers to an approach to the lifting of the veil in groups of companies. Essentially the 'enterprise entity' theory as it is sometimes termed requires the contribution of a group of companies not in terms of legal separate entities made up of parent company and subsidiaries but rather as a single business entity.

The business enterprise approach is often associated with the American academic, A. A. Berle Junior. A good judicial acknowledgement of the business enterprise approach to the idea of corporate personality can be seen in the judgment of the Ontario Court of Appeal in *Manley Inc.* v *Fallis* (1977) 38 CPR (2d) 74.

Here the defendant had set up in business in competition with the plaintiff company. The defendant's conduct would have been a breach of duty if the defendant had been a senior employee of the plaintiff company but in fact he was a senior employee of a wholly owned subsidiary of the plaintiff and the business that he had started was not in competition with that subsidiary's business.

The Ontario Court of Appeal granted an injunction in favour of the plaintiff company restraining the defendant from carrying on the business on the basis that the companies were closely related and were essentially one trading enterprise and that in the interests of the affiliated companies, a refusal of a remedy would permit the defendant to escape the consequences of his breach of a fiduciary duty.

As regards English law in *DHN Food Distributors Ltd* v *Tower Hamlets London Borough Council* [1976] 1 WLR 852 Lord Denning had adopted the position that when dealing with a group of companies such as in that case where wholly owned subsidiaries were involved the piercing of the corporate veil was possible where each of the subsidiaries were controlled by the parent and the whole group could be treated as a single economic entity.

Lord Denning's approach in the *DHN* case was following an approach he had advocated in the earlier decision of *Littlewoods Mail Order Stores Ltd* v *IRC* [1969] 1 WLR 1241. In Lord Denning's view the legislative requirement of holding companies having to prepare group accounts was an example of the law dealing with the enterprise entity and the judiciary should follow suit. This view of Lord Denning was very categorically rejected by Mason J in the High Court of Australia in *Industrial Equity Ltd* v *Blackburn* (1977) 137 LLR 567.

In the view of Mason J legislative priorities do not provide adequate justification for denying separate legal personality of each company within a group.

As far as the present position in English law is concerned one can assert that since the *DHN* case there has been a rejection of the enterprise entity. This can been seen by examining the following decisions.

Firstly the *Bank of Tokyo Ltd* decision itself. Here the Bank of Tokyo Ltd carried on a business of banking in London. Its wholly owned subsidiary Bank of Tokyo Trust Co. Ltd (BTTC) carried on a banking business in New York. Mr

Karoon was a customer of both banks. He complained that details of his account with BTTC had been disclosed by BTTC in the New York Courts for damages.

The disclosure was made for the purpose of legal proceedings in the High Court in London to which Mr Karoon and the parent company were parties. The parent company sought an order restraining the action against its subsidiary. The Court of Appeal rejected the application. In the view of the Court of Appeal, as stated in the passage of Robert Goff LJ above, in law the parent and subsidiary are distinct.

The later Court of Appeal decision of *Adams* v *Cape Industries plc* [1990] Ch 433 also shows a clear rejection of that enterprise entity approach.

In the judgment of the Court of Appeal a parent company is a distinct legal personality from its subsidiaries and this implies that each separate legal entity was complete with its own rights and liabilities.

The Court of Appeal in *Adams* had also indicated that a parent company would only be liable for acts of a subsidiary only if there is an express agency relationship. The courts have also indicated that they would not find the existence of this agency relationship merely because there is an under-capitalised subsidiary with no independent economic existence.

The finding of the agency relationship between parent and subsidiary has been utilised in the following cases. In *Smith, Stoke & Knight Ltd* v *Birmingham Corporation* [1939] 4 All ER 116 the agency relationship could be established as the subsidiary did not have any business of its own nor did the subsidiary have its own separate business premises. In the House of Lords decision of *Firestone Tyre and Rubber Co. Ltd* v *Lewellin* [1957] 1 WLR 464 the House of Lords was able to treat the parent as being the principal of the subsidiary as the facts had established a relationship of agency.

The subsidiary was part of a network of a distributorship system in the United Kingdom and Europe of the principal's goods.

It would be apparent therefore that having rejected the enterprise entity the English courts have not considered any other alternative to deal with the relationship between parent and subsidiary. As regards the agency concept the English courts have not utilised this concept to establish that liability of the parent for the debts of the subsidiary.

In contrst in the United States the courts have developed the practice of extending the veil to include the general enterprise entity such as holding affiliated transport companies liable in tort for damages caused by the negligent conduct of one of them. In *Taylor* v *Standard Gas & Electric Co.* (1939) 306 US 307, the American court held that the holding company could not prove in the bankruptcy of its subsidiary.

The judiciary in England, it is submitted, is timid in developing any principles whereby parent companies can be identified with their subsidiaries. In *Re Southard & Co. Ltd* [1979] 1 WLR 1198 Templeman LJ, as he then was, had stated that in 'English law a parent company may spawn a number of subsidiary companies, all controlled directly or indirectly, by shareholders of the parent company, and if one of the subsidiary companies were to become insolvent then the parent company would not be liable for debts of the insolvent subsidiary'.

EC Competition law, on the other hand, does treat a parent company and its subsidiaries as a single economic unit if the subsidiaries do not enjoy real autonomy in determining their course of action in the market, but carry out the instructions of the parent company which controls them. It is not certain on the present state of the English authorities whether an English court in the future would follow this approach.

In conclusion, one might state that the English courts would continue in the near future to follow the technical position of keeping the legal identity of the parent and subsidiary distinct. Certainly, *Adams* v *Cape Industries plc* demonstrates this aptly. The legislature has come to a certain extent to the assistance of creditors of subsidiaries by imposing probity on a parent company as a 'shadow director' under section 214 of the Insolvency Act 1986 and make the parent company contribute towards the assets of the insolvent subsidiary.

In *Ord* v *Belhaven Pubs Ltd* [1998] 2 BCLC 447, the Court of Appeal clearly rejected the idea of treating the group of companies as a single economic unit. In that case the Court of Appeal had held that the restructuring of a group of companies whereby assets were transferred did not involve any devious motives on the part of the directors and that the separate legal entities of the companies within a group had to be recognised. It must be noted however that the directors of a company who have removed its assets so as to defeat claims against it may be liable to the company, either for failing to fulfil their fiduciary duty to the company or under section 214 of the Insolvency Act 1986 for wrongful trading.

15 Mixed Topics

INTRODUCTION

This chapter consists of questions where what is tested is more than one area of the law. More and more exam questions involve a variety of areas so as to encourage a greater coverage of the syllabus by students.

It is advisable to read a whole question through before making a selection of questions in an exam so that you are aware of all the areas that are being tested. It is a common folly for students to read a question only superficially and then attempt it only to realise that there are issues in areas they have not revised or are inadequately prepared to deal with.

It is important to note that examiners reward mental stamina in dealing with issues systematically within the time constraints of an exam even if all the issues are not covered. Mixed area questions are ideal for testing mental stamina.

QUESTION 1

The articles of association of Dynamo Ltd are in the form of the 1985 Table A with the addition of the following provisions:

Article 65A. Any member wishing to sell his shares shall offer them to the directors who shall buy them at a fair value.

Article 65B. No shares may be offered for sale to anyone who is not a member of the company and the directors of the company may refuse to register any transfer of shares and shall not be required to furnish any reason for such refusal.

Article 89A. Any dispute arising in the internal administration of the company shall be submitted to arbitration by an arbitrator selected by the President for the time being of the Law Society.

The company was involved in property development and Henry, a shareholder, was thinking of retiring to Canada, and obtained different valuations of the company. All the valuations, although on different bases, tended to show that Henry's shares would be worth £6 per share. Henry, who held 4,000 shares, asked the directors to purchase his shares but after long negotiations was offered only £1.50 per share.

At the last annual general meeting Henry criticised the directors of the board for refusing to pay his price for the shares and alleged that the directors are 'dishonest' and unfit to be directors. The directors promptly sued him for an alleged slander. Advise Henry on (a) the disposal of his shares and (b) whether the slander allegation can be referred to arbitration.

Commentary

The question is an example of one where you have to deal with more than one topic. Here there has to be consideration of enforcement of the terms of the articles of association, particularly in relation to the transfer of shares, and the duties of directors on dealing with a transfer of shares under the articles. A remedy under section 459 of the 1985 Companies Act can also be considered.

Suggested Answer

To begin with it would be necessary to consider the issue of Henry's transfer of shares. The provision in the articles is a pre-emption right, that is, a provision that requires a member wishing to sell shares to notify the board and stating that the shares may not be offered to outsiders unless the existing members do not wish to acquire them.

'Fair Price' of the Shares

From the facts it would appear that the price that Henry has obtained seems to be independently valued and all valuations seem to show a price of £6 per share as relatively fair. The provision in the articles is quite unlike what appears in most articles of private companies, which is that a price is to be fixed by the company's auditors.

Exercise of the Directors' Powers in Relation to the Purchase of the Shares

It can be argued on behalf of Henry that the powers conferred by the articles set out the manner in which the directors have to deal with the price of the shares.

Also as held in the Court of Appeal decision of *Re Smith and Fawcett Ltd* [1942] Ch 304, any powers of the directors must be exercised bona fide in the interests of the company.

In the case of *Re Smith and Fawcett Ltd*, the provision in the articles of association conferred a wide discretionary power on directors and it was not possible for a court to substitute its standards. However, this is not the case here as the articles refer to a 'fair price'. The other point that has to be noted is that there is no question of any option on the part of the directors. So long as the price is 'fair' then directors have to purchase the shares. The offer made by the company is quite low and it is not a 'fair' price.

Action by the Member Against the Directors

The directors cannot argue that the articles relating to the sale of the shares refer to them in their capacity as 'directors' and therefore deal with outsider rights which are not enforceable by virtue of section 14 of the Companies Act 1985.

This is the case as in *Rayfield* v *Hands* [1960] Ch 1, the court held that if the directors are also shareholders, then in their capacity as members, they can be sued. This would mean that Henry can bring an action against the directors based on the breach of articles without having to join the company as a party.

It has to be also noted that the judge in *Rayfield* v *Hands* was reinforced in his interpretation by the fact that the company was a quasi-partnership, and that the acquisition of the shares pursuant to articles such as the present was in the form of one partner acquiring the shares of another.

If on the facts the directors are not shareholders, then it would appear that any action by Henry against the directors personally would fail. This is the case as they would be treated as 'outsiders' since the section 14 contract cannot bind parties other than in their capacity as members.

Rayfield v *Hands* indicates a weakness in the present form of section 14 of the Companies Act 1985, as the wording does not mention that the organs of the company including directors are also bound by the articles.

Validity of Article 65B

When Henry became a member of the company the articles of association would constitute a contract by virtue of section 14 of the Companies Act 1985. The company can thus decide whether a transfer of shares is to be permitted in favour of a person who is a non-member. The member's shareholding is thus a type of property that creates rights only so far as the articles permit.

Libel Action Brought by the Directors

The concern of Henry here would be whether he can bring about a stay of the action commenced on the basis that article 89A could be treated as a written agreement to submit differences to arbitration within section 4(1) and section 33(2) of the Arbitration Act 1950.

In *Hickman* v *Kent or Romney Marsh Sheep-Breeders' Association* [1915] 1 Ch 881, the court held that whenever an individual member is enforcing his rights as a member under the articles, then the rights would be covered by the statutory contract created by section 14. In the *Hickman* decision the particular member's dispute with the company related to being expelled from membership and was a matter that came within what is now section 14 of the 1985 Companies Act. The court granted the injunction as the agreement was a written agreement to refer matters to arbitration and so the member's action could not proceed.

The directors' allegation of slander does not seem to be a dispute between the company and its members involving membership rights. In *Wood* v *Odessa*

Water Works Co. (1889) 42 ChD 636, the court held that the articles can also constitute a contract between members themselves. Although the articles refer to disputes arising in the internal administration of the company, the slander here refers to the directors in their capacity as such and does not invoke any matters for instance that arise from the articles.

Harry would not be able to show any written agreement between himself and the directors in their capacity as such to refer matters to arbitration.

Another way in which one can consider the matter is to approach the section 14 contract by considering if Harry is enforcing a contract right that he shared in common with other shareholders. Even though the allegation was made by Harry in the course of the annual general meeting it was a personal reference to the directors and this only involves Harry and the directors.

Conclusion

Harry's remedy could include a petition under section 459 of the Companies Act 1985, on the basis that the company's failure to purchase the shares is an act that unfairly prejudices Harry in his capacity as a member, as he would not be able to realise the value of his shares. Harry's interests would otherwise be locked in the company.

QUESTION 2

The articles of association of El Key Ltd provide that 'Dennis shall be director for six years from January of 1999'. Dennis also has a contract with the company which treats him as an employee.

For the last two years Dennis was paid £10,000 per annum as his director's remuneration.

In early 1999 differences arose between Dennis and the other directors, Harry and Freddie. Harry and Freddie then arranged for shares to be issued to dilute Dennis's shareholding. Then the articles were altered to delete the provision relating to Dennis's appointment. Dennis has now been dismissed without compensation.

Discuss.

Commentary

The question requires consideration of the effect of the articles as a contract between members. There is also the issue of the company's powers in relation to the alteration of articles and the rights of directors in relation to remuneration.

Suggested Answer

In our discussion we would begin with considering whether the company is in a position to alter its articles.

Alteration of Articles

The House of Lords held in *Southern Foundries (1926) Ltd* v *Shirlaw* [1940] AC 701 that a company remains free to alter its articles and to act upon a new provision in the articles by removing a director.

The company has a legal power under section 9 of the Companies Act 1985 to alter the articles and in the *Shirlaw* case Lord Porter stated that the general principle is that a company cannot be precluded from altering its articles.

The principle referred to by Lord Porter was again cited with approval by Lord Jauncey in *Russell* v *Northern Bank Development Corporation Ltd* [1992] 1 WLR 588.

In the earlier decision of *Allen* v *Gold Reefs of West Africa Ltd* [1900] 1 Ch 656, Lindley MR had stated that since a company is empowered by statute to alter its articles from time to time any regulation or article purporting to deprive the company of this power is invalid.

Challenging the Alteration of the Articles

Although the Companies Act 1985 permits the company to alter the articles by way of a special resolution what has to be considered is whether the alteration can be said to be bona fide for the benefit of the company as a whole.

In the leading case of *Greenhalgh* v *Arderne Cinemas Ltd* [1951] Ch 286, the Court of Appeal held that the test of bona fide for the benefit of the company as a whole would be satisfied if, from the point of view of the hypothetical member, it is in the interest of the company.

Although on the facts here the allotment of additional shares would tend to show that the alteration may not be bona fide in the interest of the company, it could be argued by the majority that it would at least be of benefit to any member present or future to have a board of directors without constant conflict.

The other practical difficulty that Dennis would have is that he cannot show that there is any 'fraud on the minority' as he is not going to have his interest as a minority shareholder affected by the alteration of the articles.

Contract Between the Company and Dennis

It is possible to argue that the contract of employment incorporates as an implied term the period of six years as the period of employment. (Here there should be a discussion about implying such a term based on the *Shirlaw* case at the Court of Appeal stage.) If the articles of association were the only source of the contract then the company, as held in *Shuttleworth* v *Cox Brothers & Co. (Maidenhead) Ltd* [1927] 2 KB 9, would always be entitled to alter its articles and there would be no breach of contract. The Court of Appeal held that if contracting parties have entered into a contract on the basis of an alterable contract, the director cannot complain.

In *Southern Foundries (1926) Ltd* v *Shirlaw* [1940] AC 701, the director had been appointed for a fixed term of 10 years, not by the company's articles but by a separate contract. On our facts therefore the contract that states that Dennis is an employee would be such a contract and a term that it is for the period of six years starting from January 1999 can be implied into the contract.

Removal of Dennis under Section 303 of the Companies Act 1985

The Companies Act 1985, section 303, permits a company in general meeting by ordinary resolution to remove a director. On the authority of *Shindler* v *Northern Raincoat Co. Ltd* [1960] 1 WLR 1038, if there is a contract providing for employment for a fixed period then a resolution under section 303 would amount to a breach of contract as the resolution would constitute dismissal.

By section 303(5) of the Companies Act 1985, a company is liable to pay compensation for loss of office, on removal of a director, in the event of breach of contract.

The Amount of Compensation that Dennis Can Claim

The general position is that a director of a company does not have a right to be remunerated for any services performed for the company except as provided by its constitution or approved by the members of the company in general meeting.

In *Hutton* v *West Cork Railway Co.* (1883) 23 ChD 654, the Court of Appeal held that a director is not a servant and that the mere fact that he is acting as a director does not give him a right to be paid for it. The court then went on to state that if there are special provisions on which remuneration is paid then they have to be specifically construed.

On our facts although there is a separate contract that states that he is an employee, the contract seems to be silent on how remuneration is to be paid. In practice when the articles are in the form of Table A, article 82 provides that a director shall be entitled to such remuneration as the company may by ordinary resolution determine.

The facts indicate here that Dennis was paid £10,000 per annum as his director's remuneration in the last two years and this may be taken to be what had been agreed in general meeting or, as in *Re Duomatic Ltd* [1969] 2 Ch 365, with the unanimous assent of all members entitled to vote on the matter.

On the breach of contract on our facts, the problem would be in relation to claiming loss for the unexpired period at £10,000 per annum. This is the case as the company has not made any determination of remuneration for the unexpired period.

However, since there is a breach of contract in relation to a fixed-term contract, Dennis would be entitled to damages for wrongful dismissal.

QUESTION 3

Bob, Charles and Dexter ran a café in East London for some years on the basis of a partnership. Their accountant advised that they should continue the business through a limited company. Bob, Charles and Dexter then sought the advice of their solicitor and after a discussion it was decided that each of them should have equal numbers of shares and also there would be a provision in the company's constitution which would prevent any two getting rid of the third.

The company, Eats Ltd, was incorporated with 100 shares each issued to Bob, Charles and Dexter. The following provision was inserted in the articles: 'Where any resolution is proposed for the dismissal from the board of any director (''the threatened director'') the number of votes attached to the shares owned by the threatened director shall be equal to the number which would be required to defeat the resolution'.

Recently it has been discovered that Bob had made certain decisions committing the company to certain business transactions that caused the company a great deal of loss. It has also now come to the attention of the other directors that Bob is non-executive director of Diners Ltd which is also involved in the food and catering business and is a competitor of Eats Ltd. You have now been consulted by Charles and Dexter who want to know whether they can remove Bob from the board of directors. They are also concerned with the remedy against Bob that can be pursued by the company. Consider also what Bob's responses may be.

Commentary

The question requires the consideration of 'weighted votes' in the context of a resolution on the removal of a director. There is also a need to consider the company being a 'quasi-partnership'. The other issue that has to be considered is the nature of directors' fiduciary duties, and their enforcement.

Suggested Answer

It would be necessary to consider the powers of a company in relation to the removal of directors. Also what has to be considered is the position of articles such as in the present form that effectively prevent the company exercising the power in general meeting to remove a director.

The Company's Power to Remove a Director in General Meeting

On the facts here there is no indication of the directors being appointed by virtue of any separate contract. The appointment is by virtue of the articles, and the company need not be concerned about any liability arising from breach of contract on the company using its power of removal.

Section 303 provides a legal power to a company to remove a director by passing an ordinary resolution in general meeting. The issue that the other directors are going to be concerned with is the validity of the particular article that provides for the 'weighted votes' which effectively would prevent the passing of an ordinary resolution. The House of Lords had an opportunity to consider such a provision in the articles in the leading case of *Bushell* v *Faith*.

In *Bushell* v *Faith* the company's 300 shares were held equally between the plaintiff, the defendant and their sister. The plaintiff and defendant were the company's only directors. The company's articles weighted the voting rights attached to the shares from one per share to three per share where the issue before a general meeting of the company was the removal of the director holding those shares. The plaintiff and her sister purported to remove the defendant from his office. However, the defendant was able to defeat the resolution by the use of the 'weighted votes'.

The House of Lords, by a majority, held that the object of Parliament in passing what is today section 303 of the Companies Act 1985 was only to ensure that an ordinary resolution was to be sufficient to remove a director. The House of Lords by a majority also acknowledged that the voting rights attaching to shares when such rights are exercisable are matters for the members and the court cannot intervene since Parliament, in providing for the removal of a director by an ordinary resolution, has not considered the possibility of weighted votes.

On our facts, although the provision in the articles does not state what the number of votes are on a resolution to remove a director, the object of the article is clear and that is to use weighted votes to prevent removal. Lord Reid in *Bushell* v *Faith* was well aware that an article such as this is definitely an attempt to evade the Act, but the legislation must be construed in the light of section 303.

The directors thus must be advised that, since there is no definition of an ordinary resolution in the Companies Act 1985, a simple majority is sufficient, and in the case of any meeting of shareholders, voting powers must depend upon articles of association and the attaching of voting rights also has to be dependent on the particular articles.

The decision in *Bushell* v *Faith* is sometimes supported on the basis that the company was a quasi-partnership. On our facts it is evident that when Bob with the other directors wanted to go through incorporation they wanted to have a provision preventing the removal of each one of them as directors. The business started off as a partnership and we can say here that the characteristics of a quasi-partnership can be identfied. Lord Wilberforce in *Ebrahimi* v *Westbourne Galleries Ltd* [1973] AC 360 stated that a company would be a quasi-partnership if there is (i) an association formed or continued on the basis of a personal relationship involving mutual confidence, (ii) an agreement or understanding that all or some of the shareholders will participate in the conduct of the business, and (iii) a restriction upon the transfer of the member's interest in the company and removal from management so that he cannot take out his stake and go elsewhere.

In conclusion, therefore the provision in the articles would be enforceable and Bob would be able to defeat any resolution.

Bob Committing the Company to Business Transactions that Have Caused Losses

Bob as a director is subject to a duty to act bona fide in the interests of the company. Further he is also expected to exercise skill and care in the discharge of his duties. The decision of *Re City Equitable Fire Insurance Co. Ltd* [1925] Ch 407, has often been cited as a decision that imposes minimal standards and that a director is only liable for gross errors of judgment amounting to negligence.

The directors should be advised, however, that the decision of *Re D'Jan of London Ltd* [1993] BCC 646 has stated that the relevant test of a director's duty is not only subjective at common law but also is partly objective. The court has adopted section 214(4) of the Insolvency Act 1986 as accurately stating the law. This would mean that one is not only concerned with the general knowledge, skill and experience of the particular director but also what may be reasonably expected of a person carrying out the same functions as are carried out by that director in relation to the company. One can state that the objective standard not only applies when insolvency is predictable but also thoughout the life of the company.

So if Bob cannot be removed as a director, the company will have a cause of action against him in negligence.

Bob's Position as Director of Diners Ltd

The common law would not impose any restrictions on directors holding multiple directorships. Directors, as part of the fiduciary duties, cannot put themselves in any position where they can make a personal profit as a result of their office or any information or corporate opportunity that comes by reason of their office.

The principle is an overriding obligation adopted from the equitable obligations owed by trustees. On our facts there is no specific indication of any diversion of assets or business opportunities of Eat Ltd to Diners Ltd. However, what has to be noted is that the business decisions made by Bob and Bob's position as director of Diners Ltd does reinforce the point that the personal relationship between the shareholders has broken down.

Bob's Possible Responses

The other directors have to realise that if they attempt a removal of Bob as a director or the company takes action alleging negligence on the part of Bob then Bob could petition for a winding up of the company under section 122(1)(g) of the Insolvency Act 1986 on the grounds that it is just and equitable.

The courts are prepared to allow a winding up of a compay even if the company is relatively successful. In *Re Yenidje Tobacco Ltd* [1916] 2 Ch 426, the Court of Appeal held that if the foundation of the whole of the arrangement which the directors have entered into has failed then the court would, in view of it being contrary to good faith, permit the winding up of the company.

The other directors would find it difficult to oppose any winding-up petition on the basis of it being 'just and equitable'.

QUESTION 4

The company, Wheels Ltd is a company specialising in the sale of new and second-hand luxury cars. The members of the company are John, Henry and Imogen, who are also the directors.

During 2000 the company had taken steps to insure some of its property and a proposal form was sent to the company. John, who was managing director, signed the proposal form without reading the terms carefully. Now after fire has destroyed part of the business premises, the insurers are claiming that the risk should have been specifically notified and have denied liability.

Henry, when signing an order form relating to a supply of spare parts, agreed to accept the goods by signing it for and on behalf of 'Weels Co.'.

The transaction relating to the spare parts was not agreed to by the board of directors.

Advise the directors as to whether there is any liability on the part of John towards the company and also whether the company is liable on the contract relating to the spare parts.

Commentary

This is a question that touches on the position of directors' duty particularly in relation to skill and care. There are also aspects of agency, requiring particularly a discussion of the new section 35A of the Companies Act 1985. Finally there is a need to consider section 349 of the Companies Act 1985, an aspect that is sometimes treated as part of the area of the piercing of the corporate veil. However, it is an issue that can be tested as part of other questions.

Suggested Answer

John's Liability for Negligence

The first point to consider is the standard that the law imposes in relation to the discharge of the duties of directors. The starting-point would be the decision of *Re City Equitable Fire Insurance Co. Ltd* [1925] Ch 407. Romer J at first instance stated that the duties imposed on a director should vary according to whether one is a director of a small retail business or a director of a railway company. Romer J stated the following propositions:

(a)   A director need not exhibit in the performance of his duties a greater degree of skill than may be expected from a person of his knowledge and experience.

(b)   A director is not bound to give continuous attention to the affairs of his company.

(c)   In respect of all duties that, having regard to the exigencies of business, and the articles of association, may be left to some other official a director is, in the absence of grounds for suspicion, justified in trusting that official to perform such duties honestly.

John, it would appear, did not read the details of the proposal form, and it is a type of situation which may be considered to be something that could happen to anyone who could easily have overlooked the scope of the insurance cover.

In the years after *Re City Equitable Fire Insurance Co. Ltd*, there was a tendency to treat liability in negligence in the case of non-executive directors as only arising where there is gross negligence. However, in *Re City Equitable Fire Insurance Co. Ltd* reference was made to an earlier case of *Re Brazilian Rubber Plantations and Estates Ltd* [1911] 1 Ch 425, in which the judge had referred to a test of 'reasonable care'.

It is possible to state that there is a need to consider an objective element here. Therefore besides the three propositions stated by Romer J there is a further requirement that the director should be judged according to the manner in which a reasonable prudent person in a similar position would have acted.

In *Norman* v *Theodore Goddard* [1991] BCLC 1028, Hoffmann J, went on to state without having counsel's argument that the degree of care which a director of a company owes a duty to take when carrying out functions in relation to the company is the care that may be reasonably expected of a person carrying out those functions. In a later decision of *Re D'Jan of London Ltd* [1993] BCC 646, his lordship said that the standard of the duty of care of a director was set out in section 214(4) of the Insolvency Act 1986 and that the provision had set out correctly the common law duty of care. In *Re D'Jan of London Ltd* the court held that the director had acted negligently in not reading an insurance proposal. This position is somewhat similar to our situation here.

What is interesting about *Re D'Jan of London Ltd* is that the court only proceeded on the basis of the director's own knowledge and experience. As such there has not yet been a case which has found a director negligent on the basis of an objective test.

On our facts it appears that the insurers have repudiated liability on the basis that a specific risk should have been disclosed. It could be argued here that the director cannot be expected to display such specialist knowledge. However, objectively one may argue that the director should have sought professional advice and a prudent director would have acted in that way.

It is possible to suggest here that the courts have moved to accept a more objective test of a director's duty as to skill and care.

In practical terms neither members of companies nor liquidators would be prepared to sue directors in negligence in view of the uncertainty of the tests, even in the present state of the law.

The Contract Relating to Supply of Spare Parts

The first issue that has to be dealt with here is whether Henry has authority to bind the company. The present law has to be dealt with on the basis of section 35A of the Companies Act 1985. Section 35A now reduces the practical importance of whether Henry as director can rely on ostensible authority. Section 35A now introduces what Lord Wedderburn referred to in the House of Lords as being a 'ghost authority'. This would mean that so long as the director is able to represent the board, the directors authority is quite limitless. Therefore on our facts when Henry enters into the contract which the board is empowered to enter into section 35A now provides that so long as the third party has acted in good faith the director's powers will be free from any limitations under the company's constitution. On our facts there does not seem to be any question of the third party not acting in good faith. Section 35A(2)(c) introduces a presumption in favour of the third party as to good faith and the onus is on the company to rebut this. The provisions in section 35A implement article 9(2) of the First Company Law Directive and introduce a form of an organic theory, whereby for the first time in English law it may be possible to treat each director as representing the board of directors as an organ, instead of emphasising the agency principles or the rule in *Royal British Bank* v *Turquand* (1856) 119 ER 886.

Effects of Non-compliance with Section 349

By section 349(2) of the Companies Act 1985 if a person who is an officer of the company, such as a director like Henry, signs any order for money or goods and the company's name does not appear as required by section 351 the officer can be personally liable for the goods unless the obligation is duly paid by the company. In this case the name of 'Wheels Ltd' does not appear in the document as not only is Wheels misspelt but also 'Ltd' does not appear. In *Blum* v *OCP Repartition SA* [1988] BCLC 170, the Court of Appeal held that the omission of 'Ltd' imposed personal liability on the director.

It must be noted that the section 349 is not an instance of piercing the veil as the company can still be liable on the contract and it is only when the company fails to pay that the director would be liable.

Index